GCSE Psychology Coursework

A Practical Guide

GCSE Psychology Coursework

A Practical Guide

Jean McNiff and Mike Stanley

Hyde
Publications

First edition 1994
Reprinted 1996

Published by Hyde Publications
57, Exeter Road, Bournemouth,
Dorset BH2 5AF

ISBN 1 874154 08 2

Reprinted and bound in Great Britain by
Biddles Ltd, Guildford and King's Lynn

Contents

ACKNOWLEDGEMENTS

We wish to thank Nicky Hayes, Richard Gross and Liz Shaw for their painstaking reading of the text in draft, and for their constructive comments which have significantly strengthened aspects of the book.

We acknowledge with gratitude permission from the NEAB to reproduce the skills list on pages 9 and 10.

We thank Mr Tim Challis and the Dorset Adult Education Service for permission to reproduce the questionnaire on pages 104 and 105.

INTRODUCTION

There are a number of excellent books covering the GCSE Psychology syllabus, but very few that offer systematic guidance on doing the coursework component. We have written this book to fill the gap. The book aims to provide comprehensive and detailed advice covering all necessary aspects of psychological enquiry, methods of enquiry, data gathering, presentation and interpretation of results. It also gives useful advice on matters such as ethics in psychology, study skills, and presentation of reports in coursework. We hope that the book will help you to understand easily what you need to do in order to undertake a successful piece of coursework and to gain a good deal of enjoyment out of the exercise, as well as gain maximum marks.

The book will also help you to tackle the sections of the written examination that focus on methodology, research design, and the gathering, presentation and analysis of data. Many of the ideas addressed in this book run throughout the syllabus and provide a foundation for it.

The book is designed specifically to meet the needs of students following the NEAB syllabus. We hope that it will be helpful to students following other syllabuses, too, and that it will also offer valuable insights to students studying for 'A' and 'AS' Level courses in psychology and the social sciences.

There are worked examples of different types of coursework, and clear advice on what examination boards, and specifically the NEAB, are looking for in a well-formed piece of work.

We appreciate that people study in a variety of contexts - in schools, colleges, adult education centres and on distance learning courses. The audience for the book is wide-ranging. We have attempted to address the needs of students within the varied contexts, and we hope that you will find advice and guidance that is helpful for your particular situation.

Jean McNiff and Mike Stanley

PART 1
PREPARING

This part gives advice on getting your project work underway.

Chapter 1 explains the basic ideas of empirical research.

Chapter 2 gives detailed guidance regarding the NEAB syllabus. It spells out the do's and do not's for completing the 40 skills, with many clear examples. It shows where the skills and domains might appear in your project work.

Chapter 3 provides guidance on ethical considerations.

1 APPROACHES TO PSYCHOLOGICAL INVESTIGATION

This book is all about doing research. In your psychology textbook you have read about other people doing research. Now it is your turn. Now you are a psychological researcher in your own right.

To do psychological research you need a lively, enquiring mind, a good deal of stickability, a sound knowledge of investigative techniques, and a certain amount of ingenuity in trying them out. The first two are things that you come to on your own. Investigative and implementation techniques are procedures that you learn and practise in real life situations.

This book can give you much of the advice you need for carrying out psychological investigation, and you will find that when you start doing your own research, the ideas will fall into place. Doing psychological research means that you actively get involved in exploring ideas of your own and testing them out systematically to see if they stand up to other people's criticisms.

Empirical methods

There are different ways of doing psychological research. This book focuses on one particular way, called empirical research. The idea of empiricism is that we receive information about the world through our senses. We used empirical methods to test whether our perception of that information is trustworthy.

Empirical methods involve observing people, things and events (phenomena), formulating a hypothesis about the relationships between them, and accurately recording what we observe, with a view to drawing a conclusion that either supports or rejects our initial hypothesis. The main way in which we make sense of what we observe and record (our data) is by quantitative analysis - giving numerical values to the things and events that we observe, analysing the results through calculation, and using the resulting figures to suggest what kind of things happen (variables) and the number of times they happen (frequencies), and any trends that might be emerging between the two.

What you have to do for your practical is produce several pieces of coursework, to show how you hold some general ideas (theories) about the things people say and do. You have to articulate your ideas as more tightly formulated hypotheses. You then have to conduct systematic enquiries to show whether or not the theories and their hypotheses are acceptable, and may act as starting points for wider generalisations about the events that you are considering.

For example, let's suppose that you believe that children who receive positive feedback for socially acceptable behaviour will continue to act in the way they have been doing in order to receive the reward. You have picked up this idea from your reading of Skinner and Bowlby, amongst others, as well as from your common sense experience. You put this general idea into a more closely structured hypothesis, saying, *'Children who receive positive reinforcement through rewards for socially acceptable behaviour will repeat that behaviour.'* You then observe different situations involving some children who do and some who do not receive positive reinforcement for their behaviour: some will get gold stars at school, or praise and other encouragement at home; others will not. You compare the group that is rewarded with the group that isn't. You give a numerical value to observed incidences of their subsequent behaviour - how many correct answers a rewarded child got against how many correct answers an unrewarded child got, for example. You conduct a series of different tests in different situations to see if your comparison strengthens your case for believing that reward acts as a reinforcement to acceptable behaviour (the number of tests you run will depend on the resources available to you). If it appears that it does, then you would be justified in saying that your hypothesis was acceptable. If it appears that your initial assumptions were faulty, you would have to revise everything, including your initial assumptions.

Conducting such an enquiry may at first seem quite difficult, but as you get used to the ideas, it can be very interesting and greatly rewarding. You need to take it step by step. If you follow the advice offered in this book you won't go far wrong.

A word on terminology: people are sometimes anxious about using 'jargon'. You do not need to feel anxious. Every professional exercise has its own language. Remember what it was like when you first learned the language of computers, or cricket, for example. If you were to hold a conversation with a friend who shared these interests with you, it's unlikely that an outsider would understand what you were talking about! It is the same in psychology. There is a technical language, and you should set out to learn it and master it. You are now a psychologist in your own right, and you need to use the language in order to converse professionally with other psychologists. You need to get to grips with the language, and start talking, as well as doing, psychological research.

Note: We say 'one phenomenon' (singular)
'two phenomena' (plural).

We can use the word 'data' as singular or plural:
'data is', or 'data are'.

Good luck, and enjoy yourself!

The hypothetico-deductive method

This section involves some philosophical discussion, and is not vital for GCSE, so you can skip it if you wish. If you are interested in developing a deeper understanding into the nature of scientific enquiry, read this section. The ideas are a little hard to grasp immediately, but your efforts will be well worthwhile.

The way in which we investigate phenomena from an empirical perspective is a two-step process. First, we draw general conclusions about a phenomenon through some kind of contact with it. For example, the sun always rises in the East; water boils at a given temperature. We can see this happening. Because we observe and experience these things regularly and frequently, we come to hold a general idea about them. This process is called *induction* - the idea that we draw (induce) general laws and principles through contact with, or observation of, things and events. (Some people say this logic is mistaken. They refer to the inductivist fallacy, saying that, just because things have always happened like that, there is no guarantee that they will continue to do so. The sun may not rise in the East tomorrow. Just because water boils at 100%C, there is no guarantee that it will do so next time. Nor will we ever know, because we never actually get to the next time. When we get there, the next time has become now; so there is little likelihood that we can ever test things out to such a complete conclusion that we can say that induction is a foolproof scientific method. Accurate or not, we use induction for a geat deal of our lives: we assume that things will happen in the same way that they have always done until now.)

The second step in conducting an empirical enquiry is to work towards formulating a hypothesis, that is, an idea embodied in a statement, or theory, about the world, that aims to test some of the temporary conclusions we have drawn through the process of induction. A hypothesis is a much more tightly formulated statement than just the general hunch we might have about things because we have observed them frequently and regularly. A hypothesis states that certain relationships might hold between different things, and it acts as the starting point to a procedure that looks at those relationships in action, moves the relationships around, and sees if the conclusions are still valid. This process of forming theories and testing out our hypotheses is called *deduction*. Because we have seen things happening regularly, we believe that the order of things happens in a certain way. This provisional viewpoint is tested out so that we can have a surer foundation for offering our theory as a legitimate theory, that things actually are as we think they are.

The method of forming hypotheses, and then testing them out via a scientific investigation is often called *'the hypothetico-deductive method'*: we form a hypothesis and then systematically test it out to see if it holds water or not.

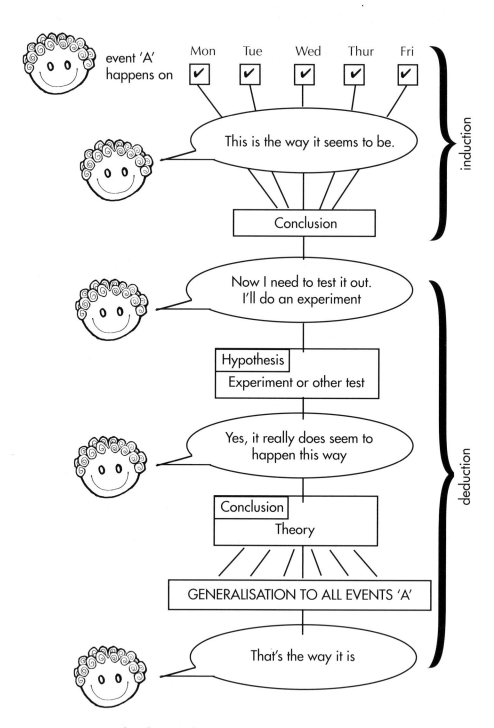

The hypothetico-deductive method

2 THE NEAB SYLLABUS

In following the NEAB coursework requirements you are using mainly empirical methodologies - that is, you are aiming to observe and describe the things that people say and do, to test out some theories you have about those things, and to draw some conclusions about them that may be applicable to the wider field of human thought and action. You are not aiming necessarily to bring about any kind of change in the situation you are studying.   What the examination is testing is that you are able to demonstrate a clear understanding of the empirical methods of social scientific enquiry by using those methods to carry out some pieces of coursework of a reasonably limited and focused nature.

The value of coursework

All GCSE Psychology courses contain a coursework component usually worth 20% of the total marks available. This may not seem a lot compared to the 80% awarded for the written examination but it can make a significant difference to your final GCSE grade. For example, a candidate who earns 115 out of 160 marks on the two written papers for one major examination board (worth a grade C) produces a folder of coursework worth 40 marks (20%), then qualifies for a grade A. Even more dramatically, a candidate who doesn't do very well in the written examination, earning say 59 out of 160 (grade F), could convert this to a grade C by producing an excellent project folder. It is worth taking the time and trouble over coursework which has the advantage of not being done under stressful examination conditions.

How to earn the most from your coursework

The following advice is based on the requirements of the NEAB, although it stands as good practice for all psychology practical work at this level.

Practical work forms an essential part of GCSE Psychology, and teachers are required to record in positive terms the achievements of their students. Many of the skills required for coursework are also tested on the written papers and it is hoped that practical work will serve to reinforce those skills and abilities needed to enable a full understanding of the theoretical aspects of psychological methods and techniques.

Six Domains have been identified by the NEAB, and there is a total of 40 skills to be earned. The total for the coursework component is 20% of the whole examination, so each skill carries $1/2$%. Each skill has to be demonstrated correctly only once to be credited and so it doesn't matter how many times you get it wrong, as long as you eventually get it right at least **once**. This is the advantage of *positive* marking.

The GCSE course aims to make candidates aware of a range of investigative techniques open to psychologists. Indeed, some of the 40 skills relate to experimental investigations, others to observational studies and to surveys. Ideally this means that to stand the best chance of gaining all 40 marks, your coursework folder should contain **three** investigations:

1 an experiment
2 an observational study
3 a survey (using a questionnaire)

It is certainly **not** recommended for candidates to attempt to demonstrate these skills in one long investigation. This is fraught with dangers and in the past many students have had marks deducted for not adequately demonstrating all the skills in a single study.

On the other hand, there are other ways in which some of the skills may be demonstrated - particularly for students who are on short courses (one year) and don't have the time to produce three investigations. Some teachers opt to set their students a series of worksheets in which they answer questions relating to some of the skills. Although this is not ideal, it is permissible for **some** of the skills to be assessed. However, if this is employed, it is still essential for at least **one** investigation to be carried out following the accepted conventions for writing up projects (see Chapter 13). The NEAB suggests that it will be found necessary for at least two investigations to be carried out for all the skills to be covered.

In order to ensure that the time spent writing up projects is not excessive, it is recommended that the report of a single investigation should not exceed 1,000 words (see Chapter 14).

Remember that candidates must prove to a coursework moderator that they understand and can demonstrate these skills. The examination board regards most of the 40 skills as 'preservable', which means that they are available for inspection in the coursework folder. It is your job to prove that you have acquired the skills. It will not be assumed if it is not there in writing for the moderator to see.

It should go without saying that candidates are forbidden to indulge in any unfair practice in carrying out practical work, but it is surprising how some students unwittingly do this from time to time. Before embarking on project work, it is worth being absolutely sure of what you can and cannot do to avoid falling into this trap, because if the examination board thinks that an offence has been committed, the candidate will be liable to disqualification in extreme circumstances. Undoubtedly the most common offence is submitting work which is not the individual work of the candidate. In other words, what you submit **must be entirely your own work**. This does not preclude assessments being made on practical work carried out as a group activity, but where group work is used, it must be absolutely clear what the contribution made by a particular student is and assessed accordingly. This is most likely to affect the skills awarded in Domain A (Planning Investigations). We shall say more about this aspect later.

There are generally accepted conventions for writing up practical work in psychology, and following them will help you to make sure of the six domains of skills outlined in the NEAB syllabus. Detailed advice on these matters will be given in Part Five.

Skills to be tested

Here is the list of skills.

SKILLS			Mark 1, 0 or ABS (see paras. 28 and 42 of Instructions)	Page no. of report (see para. 29 of Instructions)	Date of achieve-ment
Domain A: Planning investigations					
	A1	formulate and state an hypothesis?			
	A2	identify the independent variable?			
	A3	identify the dependent variable?			
	A4	identify extraneous variables?			
Is the	A5	suggest ways to control extraneous variables?			
candidate	A6	choose an appropriate experimental design?			
able to	A7	justify choice of experimental design?			
	A8	select appropriate sampling technique?			
	A9	consider the availability of resources?			
	A10	select appropriate materials/apparatus?			
	A11	devise appropriate experimental procedures?			
	A12	devise categories for describing behaviour?			
Domain B: Implementation					
	B1	select/recruit suitable subjects?			
	B2	administer standardised instructions?			
	B3	de-brief subjects?			
	B4	construct a record sheet?			
Is the	B5	construct a questionnaire?			
candidate	B6	pilot a questionnaire?			
able to	B7	carry out procedures systematically?			
	B8	handle materials/subjects safely?			
	B9	make accurate measurements/observations?			
	B10	assign behaviour to categories?			
Domain C: Recording and processing data					
	C1	record data in appropriate forms?			
Is the	C2	head tables correctly?			
candidate	C3	choose an appropriate graphical scale?			
able to	C4	label the axes of graphs?			
	C5	plot graphs, bar charts and histograms?			
Domain D: Processing of data					
Is the	D1	identity anomalous results?			
candidate able to	D2	perform calculations on the data?			

SKILLS		Mark 1, 0 or ABS (see paras. 28 and 42 of Instructions)	Page no. of report (see para. 29 of Instructions)	Date of achieve- ment
Domain E: Interpreting data				
	E1 recognise patterns in data?			
	E2 deduce relationships between variables?			
	E3 critically consider the data?			
Is the candidate able to	E4 explain variability in data?			
	E5 draw conclusions/generalisations?			
	E6 explain data in psychological terms?			
	E7 suggest improvements to method?			
	E8 relate findings to other investigations?			
Domain F: Reports				
Is the candidate able to	F1 include all major aspects?			
	F2 present material clearly?			
	F3 avoid repetition and irrelevancy?			
	Total raw mark (max. 40)			

Scaled total mark (max. 80) (multiply total raw mark x 2)		(A)
Spelling, punctuation and grammar mark (max. 4)		(B)
Overall total mark (max. 84)		(A + B)

Domains

You will see that the list of skills are broken down into six Domains, each of which tests different aspects of enquiry. What follows here is a brief overview of examination requirements. Amplification follows in later chapters.

Domain A: Planning Investigations

This section tests your ability in planning and designing your projects. You need to be familiar with the methods, techniques and principles appropriate for ensuring objectivity, such as population sampling, using standardised procedures, understanding the idea of variables and how they may be manipulated.

Domain B: Implementation

This section tests your ability to decide on suitable ways for conducting experimental and field investigations. You need to find out how to devise questionnaires and record sheets, observe, conduct interviews, and be sensitive to the needs of other people involved in your study.

Domain C: Recording and Presentation of Data

In this section you need to show that you can record and present your data in a clear and unambiguous visual form, so that people will be able to understand exactly what information you are aiming to communicate.

Domain D: Processing the Data

You need to show your understanding of basic descriptive statistical concepts, perform some simple calculations, and identify any results that are in some way out of the ordinary (anomalous).

Domain E: Interpreting the data

This section gives you an opportunity to discuss your study, to show trends and patterns, and to draw reasonable inferences in terms of how you think the aspects you are studying might continue to develop: for example, if you are studying the effect of auditory interference on memory, what are the implications for how you organise your own study time so that you can remember facts most efficiently? The section also gives you an opportunity to evaluate your work and say how you might improve the study if you did it again. You should also aim to show how your study relates to the wider literature - books, reports, newspaper and magazine articles, and so on.

Domain F: Reports

This section examines the overall quality of your study and how you report it. One of the most important criteria for doing and reporting empirical research is whether it can be replicated - that is, if I read your report, will I be able to do your study again myself, and will my data yield fairly similar results? Domain F skills test whether the study is written following accepted conventions in a clear and unambiguous way.

The following table is a rough guide to where you are most likely to demonstrate the 40 skills (see also Chapter 13):

Skills	Location
Domain A (except A10)	Introduction
Domain B (plus A10)	Method: subjects apparatus procedure
Domains C and D	Results
Domain E	Discussion
Domain F	The whole report

We stated earlier that it is virtually impossible to show all 40 skills in one project. You should aim to present three projects (two plus additional exercises is permissible). Here is a rough guide to the skills the examiners would expect to find in each project. Please note that it is possible to attempt some skills up to three times, but others are only possible once. Therefore you may decide (if you are not happy with the marks you have earned) to re-write some of your coursework. You must negotiate this with your teacher.

Skills	Project		
	Observation	Questionnaire	Experiment
A1	✔	✔	✔
A2			✔
A3			✔
A4	✔	✔	✔
A5	✔	✔	✔
A6			✔
A7			✔
A8	✔	✔	✔
A9	✔	✔	✔
A10	✔	✔	✔
A11			✔
A12	✔		
B1	✔	✔	✔
B2		✔	✔
B3		✔	✔
B4	✔	✔	✔
B5		✔	
B6		✔	
B7	✔	✔	✔
B8	✔	✔	✔
B9	✔		✔
B10	✔		
C1	✔	✔	✔
C2	✔	✔	✔
C3	✔	✔	✔
C4	✔	✔	✔
C5	✔	✔	✔
D1	✔	✔	✔
D2	✔	✔	✔
E1	✔	✔	✔
E2	✔	✔	✔
E3	✔	✔	✔
E4	✔	✔	✔
E5	✔	✔	✔
E6	✔	✔	✔
E7	✔	✔	✔
E8	✔	✔	✔
F1	✔	✔	✔
F2	✔	✔	✔
F3	✔	✔	✔

It is good advice to leave the experiment to the last. Use the other two investigations to develop your skills of presenting coursework. You will probably find that you are better equipped to tackle the Domain E skills in the latter half of the course when you have more knowledge of experiments done by psychologists.

It is recognised that within each Domain, some tasks are more demanding than others. Certain of the skills involve higher order abilities which will be achieved by only a proportion of candidates. This is particularly so for Domain E skills. It is anticipated that all candidates will be able to master certain skills, but that others, although able to show some degree of competence, will not reach the standard for a mark to be awarded. However, it is not unreasonable to expect a grade A candidate to achieve the maximum of 40 marks (the full 20%) for coursework.

Demonstrating the skills

Let's look now at each of the 40 skills. They are identified on the assessment form which will be attached to your project folder, but it is worth asking your teacher for a copy of this at the start of the course. We shall amplify each skill for you and give examples of how they may be shown. Each example provided did actually earn marks for students in previous years. All aspects which are briefly presented here will be explained thoroughly in later chapters.

Domain A: Planning Investigations

A1   Formulate an hypothesis

The study may be concerned with differences or relationships and the hypothesis must be clear about this. Some candidates make the mistake of stating a general aim rather than formulating a specific hypothesis. For example, an hypothesis for an experiment should express the effects which proposed changes in the independent variable would have on the dependent variable. If you were investigating perceptual set, a suitable hypothesis would be *'Previous experience will affect perception of an ambiguous figure'*.

A2   Identify the independent variable

It must be clear in your writing that you understand that the independent variable is the variable which the experimenter is to manipulate. Then you must identify it. If the experiment on perceptual set used Leeper's ambiguous lady, you would say, *'The independent variable is the young or old lady'*.

A3   Identify the dependent variable

Make it clear that you know that the dependent variable is the variable which is to be measured. However, it is not good enough to say that the dependent variable is 'the results'. This will not earn the skill mark. It is better to say, *'The dependent variable is the type of lady seen'*.

A4   Identify extraneous variables

It is dangerous just to throw in terminology without attempting to show that you understand what it means. Candidates often do this when addressing this skill. You need to show that you understand that extraneous variables, if not controlled, could affect the outcome of the investigation. This is a planning skill and should be demonstrated in the planning stage of the study (i.e. the introduction) and not in the subsequent discussion following execution of the study, as candidates sometimes do. In previous years, some candidates have identified age and sex of participants as extraneous variables, despite using a repeated measures design, not seeming to realise that repeated measures design controls individual differences which therefore are NOT extraneous variables. Order effects would be more appropriate in these situations. In the case of memory tasks, you might suggest noise or other environmental factors that could affect concentration. In each study, try to suggest at least two important variables which need to be controlled. There are usually plenty of things to choose from - think of experimenter effects and timing problems, for example.

A5   Suggest ways to control extraneous variables

Make sure you have identified variables that can be controlled, and then suggest sensible ways in which this can be done. It is not enough to say, 'These are beyond the control of the experimenter.' There are plenty of things you can do. For example, order effects could be dealt with by counterbalancing (explain what this means as well), or experimenter effects might be controlled by having standardised instructions.

A6   Choose a suitable experimental design

You must decide between repeated measures, matched subjects and independent measures, explaining what this entails: for example, *'The design used was independent measures as each research participant performed only in one condition.'*

A7   Justify choice of experimental design

You must give reasons for your chosen design. It is not enough to say, *'I used a repeated measures design because I thought it was best.'* It may be appropriate for you to say why other designs were not chosen within your justification. For example, in the perceptual set experiment, *'A repeated measures design could not be used because participants' responses in the second condition would be affected by their experience of the first condition. An independent measures design would be best because with participants working only in one condition, there will be nothing to bias their response apart from the independent variable.'*

A8   Select appropriate sampling technique

Don't be misled into believing that you must say 'random' sampling. Many candidates have said this in the past and lost the skill mark because their sampling technique clearly wasn't random. It is very difficult to achieve random sampling and it will probably be more appropriate to employ a different method. Decide which method of sampling is most suitable and say why. It is quite acceptable to choose opportunity sampling, provided you make it clear that you understand what it is and why it is necessary. For example, *'We were only able to conduct this experiment in the college refectory at lunch time and therefore had to settle for anyone who came along and would agree to take part. This is known as opportunity sampling.'*

A9   Consider the availability of resources

This is a planning skill different to simply listing the materials needed (which is A10). Apart from obtaining the apparatus you need, don't forget that time and participants are also resources. Here it is quite appropriate to discuss the allocation of time to tasks and the most appropriate sampling technique given the scarce resources available, such as participants.

A10   Select suitable materials/apparatus

This is probably one of the easiest skills to earn, but make sure that you don't leave anything essential out of the list. If it is clear that you are running a timed investigation, we would expect to see a timing device mentioned in the apparatus section.

A11   Devise appropriate experimental procedures

This is where you state your intentions for running the experiment. The emphasis is on **devising** procedures and should not be confused with skills B2 and B7. Here you can point out the need for standardised instructions to minimise the risk of experimenter effect on participants' performance. However, standardised instructions should be documented verbatim (see Skill B2).

A12   Devise categories for describing behaviour

This skill belongs to the observation study and should contain discrete (separate) categories of behaviour that can be observed and recorded by a tally method. This mark cannot be earned by analysing participants' responses to a questionnaire and categorising their answers. There are plenty of interesting ideas for simple observation studies listed in the GCSE syllabus. Be careful not to use categories where you are making assumptions about what someone is thinking. You can only note what you see. Therefore 'was happy' and 'was angry' are not good categories, but 'smiled' and 'frowned' are fine.

Domain B: Implementation

B1   Select and recruit suitable subjects*

Simply say how many people were obtained, how many males and females, age range (mean age if possible), and how they were chosen.

---

*The NEAB still uses the word 'subjects' on its Candidate Internal Assessment Form. This is about to be revised.

B2 Administer standardised instructions

This mark will not be awarded for the statement, '*Standardised instructions were administered*'. Simply pointing out that there are written instructions at the top of the questionnaire will NOT earn the mark. **What you say to your participants is important here**. Use quotation marks to make it absolutely clear **what was said to the participants**. Remember to include the script in your project.

B3 De-brief subjects

This has always been an important issue but even more so now that new ethical guidelines have been published (see Chapter 3). It is important for participants to know the true purpose of the investigation and the part they played. Obviously it is polite to thank them, but by simply stating 'participants were thanked', you will not earn the mark. It is good practice to have a de-briefing script included in your report.

B4 Construct a record sheet

In the past, some candidates have not appeared to understand the difference between a record sheet and tables. It is intended that a record sheet be used as a primary point of data collection where the raw data can be recorded. A table is a record of the collection or summary of these data. You must distinguish between these two types of data recording. In Chapter 7 we look at the construction of record sheets, and in Chapter 11 we look at tables and other ways of presenting the data.

B5 Construct a questionnaire

If you decide to construct a questionnaire as a group project, you must document your individual contribution to such a questionnaire. If this is not made clear, both you and your partners are in danger of losing this skill mark.

B6 Pilot a questionnaire

Don't confuse this skill with 'conducting a pilot study'. What you should do for this mark is devise a pilot questionnaire, administer it to a small number of participants, and then analyse the responses to identify ambiguous questions or other items. These questions should then be rephrased or omitted when the final version of the questionnaire is produced. You must document this process and include copies of the pilot questionnaire and final draft as appendices to the report. Simply saying, 'We piloted the questionnaire' will not earn the skill mark.

B7 Carry out procedures systematically

This mark is awarded for the 'procedure' section. It should be written in sufficient detail to permit replication of the investigation.

B8   Handle materials/subjects safely

Here is a good opportunity to demonstrate your knowledge of ethical issues. You could make it clear in your procedure that you are not putting participants under undue stress. Also you could reassure participants that the results will be anonymous and that they may withdraw from the study at any point.

B9   Make accurate measurements/observations

A table of figures of accurate measurements collected during the study earns this mark.

B10   Assign behaviour to categories

This skill is associated with skill A12 and refers to the process of carrying out an observation study. You should use a recognisable on-going counting method (e.g. tallying using the five-bar gate ⅢⅠ). Include this record sheet in your project as an appendix to be sure of earning this mark.

Domain C: Recording and processing data

C1   Record data in appropriate forms

There are various ways to earn this skill mark. Tables of figures, charts and graphs may all be appropriate ways of presenting data. Be careful not to present line graphs when dealing with discrete data. This is not appropriate and you should understand the distinction between discrete and continuous data and how to record it graphically.

C2   Head tables correctly

Headings on tables should state what the information in the table is describing. The units of measurement should be made clear. Some candidates head tables simply with the words 'Table of results'. This will **not** earn the skill mark. Only when the heading specifically describes the data contained in the table will the mark be awarded. For example, *'Table to show the number of words correctly recalled in both conditions'* would be acceptable. Don't be afraid to write a long heading.

C3   Choose an appropriate graphical scale

Graphs should be done on graph paper and sensible use should be made of this paper. Marks will not be awarded for graphs drawn on plain or lined paper. In your folder of coursework at least one graph should be hand drawn to be sure of earning this skill mark. Many students now have word processors which can produce very impressive graphs. However, we are not assessing the skills of your word processor. We want to know what **you** can do.

C4   Label the axes of graphs

Just having numbers up the side of a graph is not good enough. The labels must also be there; for example, 'number of words recalled'. Also, don't forget to give your graph a title.

C5   Plot graphs, bar charts and histograms

Any correctly plotted graph will carry this mark. Usually, coursework moderators will look to see if the graphs correctly match tables of figures - so don't be careless plotting points!

Domain D: Processing of data

D1   Identify anomalous results

Point out results which may be either abnormally high or low or which do not fit into a pattern. For example, *'A few anomalous results could have affected the outcome. Participant 1 had both scores much lower than average, especially on list B with only 11 words recalled. This might distort the mean.'* Alternatively, there might genuinely be no anomalous results. Provided you make it clear that you understand this, it is quite acceptable to say, *'There were no abnormally high or low results in the data - in other words, there were no anomalous results.'* Provided this is true, you should earn the mark.

D2   Perform calculations on the data

You must perform at least two types of calculation in your coursework but they need not be in the same project. Remember that inferential statistics are not required in GCSE Psychology and therefore don't qualify for this mark, unless it is clear within the work that you have calculated a mean, median, range, percentage or ratio (any two).

Domain E: Interpreting data

E1   Recognise patterns in data

Any patterns which arise (even unexpected patterns) can be described here. They can refer to linear relationships (as in a correlation study) or differences (as in an experiment). Use the figures to support your statement. For example, *'The average number of words recalled with category headings was 20.9 which is higher than the average number of words recalled without category headings, which was 15.3. This shows that category headings are an aid to recall.'*

E2   Deduce relationships between variables

Here you must relate the results to the hypothesis under test. But it is not enough simply to say, 'The results supported the hypothesis'. You must provide amplification to gain the mark. For example, *'The hypothesis "Category headings will increase the number of words recalled compared to words being recalled with no headings" was supported because the results show that the average number of words recalled with headings was greater than the average number recalled without headings by 5.6.'*

E3   Consider data critically

You should consider how the data were affected by limitations. Here you can consider a range of possibilities from environmental factors (e.g. *'working in the refectory was not an ideal place as some subjects were distracted more than others. This could have had an effect on the outcome'*), to procedural problems (e.g. *'We allowed subjects too much time to learn the words and some achieved perfect scores'*), to materials used (e.g. *'Some of the words chosen might have been more difficult to learn than others and this could have affected the results'*).

E4   Explain variability in data

Consider the range of scores and offer explanations for these differences. You could focus on individuals; for example, *'Person 12 must have had a very good memory as recall was high in both conditions (22 on list A and 20 on list B)'*, or make more general points such as, *'In both conditions the females seemed to perform better than the males, probably because they took it more seriously. The males tended to fool around a lot because the experimenters were female and they were showing off,'* or *'The people who did better said they tried to use the words to make up a story and this helped them to remember more.'*

E5   Draw conclusions/generalisations

Can you confidently draw conclusions and make generalisations from your study? Write something like this: *'From our results it would appear that people do remember more words when provided with headings.'* But don't make sweeping generalisations, such as *'Our study demonstrates that there is a definite link between ... '* or *'Our study proves ... '*. You can't prove anything in life; all you can do is draw reasonable inferences, and then you still have to be a bit cautious.

E6   Explain data in psychological terms

Many candidates go to great lengths in their introductions to provide background information to their studies, quoting theory and research. However, this will not earn the mark unless **in the discussion** they attempt to apply these explanations to the results they have gained. For example, *'Our results show that category headings are an aid to recall a list of words. This is because category headings act as a cue and help to organise information in memory and so produce more recall.'*

E7   Suggest improvements to method

The most popular offering here is, *'We should use more participants.'* This does not impress coursework moderators unless you can suggest a good reason why more participants are necessary. Better candidates carefully consider improvements to the design of the study. It may even be worth looking back to what you said for skill E3 for clues to improvements. For example, *'It might have been better to use an independent measures design, making it possible to use the same words in both conditions,'* or *'We might have been able to sort out better timings by conducting a pilot study before the main study.'* Try to offer at least two good improvements.

E8   Relate findings to other investigations

Once again, even if you have mentioned other investigations in your introduction, you will not earn this mark unless you apply the findings of these investigations when discussing the results of your own study. For example, *'We achieved similar results to Tulving and Pearlstone (1966). Their participants memorised a list of words. When they had to recall the list, half of the people were given sheets of paper with category headings printed on and the other half just had blank paper. The group with category headings recalled many more words than the group who didn't have them.'*

Domain F: Reports

This domain relates to the presentation of your coursework folder.

F1   Include all major aspects

At least one report must follow the conventional format, organised under the following headings:

Introduction
Method
Results
Discussion
Conclusion

F2   Present material clearly

Obviously your writing must be legible and comprehensible. Read it through yourself before submitting it. Can **you** understand it?

F3   Avoid repetition and irrelevancy

Weaker candidates often say the same thing over and over again or just waffle. The procedure section should not be a repetition of the introduction and the discussion should not be the procedure written in the past tense. Each section should add a new dimension to the whole report.

> If you follow this advice carefully and conscientiously, you stand every chance of gaining full marks for your coursework.

3 ETHICAL CONSIDERATIONS

In Charles Kingsley's book 'The Water Babies' there is a character called 'Mrs Doasyouwouldbedoneby'. She captures the idea of ethical thought and action.

There are specific ethical guidelines available from the British and American Psychological Societies, and the document *Ethics in Psychological Research: Guidelines for students at pre-degree levels* (January, 1992) is available from the Association of Teachers of Psychology, c/o The British Psychological Society, St. Andrew's House, 48 Princess Road East, Leicester, LE1 7DR. This document is very helpful, and contains advice on the do's and don't's of psychological research, such as

'You should **never**

- insult, offend or anger participants
- make participants believe that they have harmed or upset someone else
- break the law or encourage others to do so
- contravene the Data Protection Act
- illegally copy tests or materials
- make up data
- copy other people's work
- claim that somebody else's wording is your own'

Everyone engaged in psychological research at any level should be familiar with these guidelines. You must be aware of what you can and cannot do when conducting investigations. What seems harmless and good fun to eager students can cause distress and even danger to poor unsuspecting participants. You should gain approval for conducting your investigation from your teacher.

Extreme cases of unethical practice could result in disqualification from the examination. Fortunately these are very rare.

General issues about ethics in psychological investigation

Here are some of the most common points.

Subjects or participants?

As a researcher in a democratic and humanitarian society you need to show care and respect to others. This is what you would expect from them. An implication is whether you would regard the people taking part in your study as subjects or participants - that is, are you doing research ON them or WITH them? Current practice amongst examining boards and psychological associations, such as the British Psychological Society, is to stop using the word 'subjects', as has been common practice in psychological investigation, and instead use 'participants'. You will notice that the NEAB skills list still occasionally uses the word 'subjects', but in 1996 this will be replaced with the word 'participants'. You should aim to use 'participants' at all times.

Ethical practice tells us that, even though we might 'use' people as the objects of our enquiries, they are still individual persons, and we must protect them from our own possible unthinking insensitivity when doing research.

Deception

Some psychologists make a convincing case for the need for deception. If people actually knew why they were doing an experimental task, they argue, their behaviour might be influenced, and the results might be distorted. For example, if you wanted to investigate people's attitudes towards certain sensitive social issues - say the entitlement of minority interest groups such as women - you might present the ideas wrapped up in another form. You might, for example, conduct a survey of shop assistants, male and female, to ask them about customer behaviour towards them. They would think you were investigating customer behaviour; secretly you would be gathering data on attitudes towards male and female shop assistants. Some researchers would argue that it is acceptable to maintain secrecy. Others would argue strongly that even this level of deception is unethical. Good practice says that the very least the researcher should do is to take the client into her or his confidence after the interview or form-filling session, and explain what the research is all about - and also explain the reasons for the secrecy. Some psychologists and social scientists would suggest that deception is always unnecessary.

De-briefing is tested at Skill B3; general ethical practice is tested at skill B8. It is not enough in your report to say, 'I thanked my subjects/participants and de-briefed them.' You must indicate what that means: '*I thanked each participant personally, and explained to them the purpose of my investigation and the contribution they had made to its success*', and any further elaboration that you feel is necessary. The script used to convey this information should be included in your report.

The right to refuse

You must never force people into doing anything. If they hesitate at your request to take part in your investigation, you must not use any form of pressure. This means that friends must be left in peace if they say they do not want to join your group to test visual perception (Susan is slightly colour-blind and is sensitive to what is an acceptable condition in her life but which other people in the past have found amusing); people must not be badgered in the street to answer your questionnaire (Mr Smith likes to do the shopping to get some peace and quiet, and he does not want to be disturbed by insistent researchers). If people refuse to take part, their wishes must be respected. If they initially agree to take part, but then wish to leave the investigation, you must allow them to do so with absolute good grace, not with an implied grumble or feeling of resentment.

Non-participant observation

The considerations of respect for people's privacy and right to refuse may be relaxed in non-participant observations, provided that the people observed are not later identified and confronted with their behaviour. If, for example, you want to count the number of people travelling alone in cars along your road, it would be very difficult to let them all know that you were there and watching them. You would be counting heads, rather than observing people. In this case their privacy is not being invaded. How many times have you and I appeared in holiday photographs and videos? It is one of the facts of living in today's technological society that we are recorded, photographed and otherwise captured electronically. That is the rationale for the Data Protection Act: to protect people from the abuse of data about them that is stored in private and public data retrieval systems. However, if you wish to focus on individuals' behaviour as a non-participant, you must be very careful not to invade their right to privacy. It would be most unethical, for example, to carry a tape recorder in your pocket to record people's comments without first asking their permission, or to set up a videocamera to videotape them without their knowledge; or to indulge in notorious practices such as observing people from a cubicle in a public toilet.

Confidentiality, privacy and anonymity

It is absolutely vital to maintain confidentiality at all times. You must assure the people taking part in the investigation that you will not disclose their identity and that you will preserve their privacy and dignity at all costs. When you come to writing up your report, if you have to name people, use their initials, or even make up the initials or alternative names, or allocate them numbers, such as 'Participant 8'. If you assure them of confidentiality, keep your word. Do not then talk about people to others.

Avoid causing stress, discomfort or embarrassment

Remember, do as you would be done by. People who tell jokes with a sting in the tail think the joke is very funny, until they are the butt themselves. Then it is not so funny. Whatever you ask people to do in your investigation, make sure that you are not causing them present or future stress.

Recent examples of studies considered unethical were those relating to the use of taboo words in a perceptual defence experiment. Even though this is referred to in a popular GCSE textbook, it would now be unwise to attempt it. Also, experiments involving the use of damaging substances such as alcohol would be seen as unethical even if the participants are over eighteen. Don't forget - these people will probably have to get home after your experiment and if they are driving, you could be responsible for a nasty accident.

Animals in psychological investigations

As you read your textbooks you will come across horror stories of how psychologists have used and abused animals in their investigations. Some students find it difficult to get past the feelings of anger and revulsion that such reports engender to get through to the implications for psychological enquiry. On the other hand, you might feel that the use of animals is justified in psychological research, such as in medical aspects. Whatever you believe, you have a right to your opinion, though you do not have a right to impose it on others. You also have a moral duty to ensure that your opinion is based on sound critical reasoning and humane awareness; and you have an intellectual duty to be ready to state the reasons for your beliefs if you are asked for justification.

You must not employ animals in your projects in any sense where you may be seen to be exploiting the animal or abusing its rights to lead a peaceful and dignified life. You may investigate the use of animals in areas of life where the quality of the animal's life is being improved. For example, a kind of research in which animals are employed is currently enjoying much publicity and approval. This is the area in which animals work with humans for their mutual benefit - for example, guide dogs, 'hearing' dogs, pets for the disabled, lonely, and emotionally disturbed. Animals clearly enjoy the care and attention they receive, and people benefit from the sharing of love.

You may do research **WITH** animals, in this mutually beneficial sense; but you may **NOT** do research **ON** animals. In practice, this will probably mean that you may do an observational study of animal behaviour, or people and their pets, but under no circumstances should you attempt an experiment using animals.

PART 2
PLANNING YOUR RESEARCH PROJECT

This part contains chapters 4 and 5, to do with the practical and scientific considerations in planning a research project.

In planning your project, ask yourself the following questions:

What am I going to study?
Who am I going to study?
How am I going to study this?
What sort of evidence can I gather or produce? How will I make sense of that evidence?

What am I going to study?

This question will focus your attention on the practical issues of what your study context is, what you are interested in, or able to study, and keeping a fairly narrow focus throughout the course of your study. The scientific issues involved will concern the idea of variables.

How do I want to study this?

This question will require you to address the practical issues of choice of methodology and design. The scientific considerations will require you to have a working knowledge of different kinds of experimental designs, how to choose them and how to use them.

Who do I want to study?

This question makes us think about the practical issues of considering the availability and suitability of resources, including people. The scientific considerations will require us to be familiar with sampling techniques, so that we will be able to choose and use our resources as best suits our chosen methodology.

What sort of evidence can I gather? How will I make sense of that evidence?

Practical issues here involve the kinds of organisation we can employ to gather and store our data. Scientific implications are the ways in which we gather and analyse our data.

Chapter 4 offers advice on the practical considerations involved in asking these four questions.

Chapter 5 offers advice regarding the scientific criteria involved in answering the questions.

4 PLANNING YOUR PROJECT: PRACTICAL CONSIDERATIONS

1 Asking the right questions

(a) What am I going to study? - Choosing a topic

Some teachers help their students by organising a class project. In this case you will probably not have a choice of topic. The teacher will set the area to be studied, arrange discussion about appropriate methodology, show you how to gather data and analyse it, and generally monitor your progress. The cover sheet at the front of your project indicates what help you were given in carrying out your investigation. However, you will have to do the actual project work yourself. The writing up of your investigation, your interpretations and conclusions, must all be your own original work.

If the project is directed by somebody else, it could prevent you from earning some skills in Domain A, so many teachers recommend that students choose at least one topic of their own to enable them to demonstrate the skills in Domain A. Many students, particularly mature learners, often prefer this, on the grounds that they are selecting an area that is of particular interest or concern to them; and they tend to feel a sense of ownership and personal empowerment if they decide what they wish to study. It is entirely up to the teacher and students to negotiate their learning strategy: how the project work is conducted, the organisation of group or independent study, study schedules, and so on.

If you are in the position of choosing your own topic (such as if you are working in an independent or distance-learning mode), there are certain points you need to remember:

Start small

You are aiming to spend about 50-60 hours on your project work altogether. You have not the time nor resources to follow through an elaborate study. What you need to do is fulfil the 40 specified criteria.

You should not, therefore, feel that you have to tackle a large-scale topic such as investigating the relationship between watching violence on television and aggressive behaviour among teenagers, or the effect of sibling rivalry on examination success. This kind of issue is very interesting, and certainly needs to be investigated; but it is outside the scope of GCSE work. You need to focus on something quite small such as whether interference affects a simple memory test, or what people's attitudes are towards a particular issue.

Keep focused

Right at the beginning of your study you need to decide on your hypothesis, or the objectives of your study. Sometimes students start their project with only a half-formed idea of exactly what it is they wish to study. They tend to amass a quantity of data but are then uncertain what to do with it. Making the project up as you go along may be good fun, but it can also be wasteful of time and energy. It is much more cost-effective to invest time in planning in some detail what you want to study and how you are going to do this.

Keep in touch with your teacher here, and with your fellow students. Your teacher might ask you to rough out an action plan for your topic and for your own time-management (see below). It is a good idea to keep a workbook handy at all times, and to write down ideas as they form. Writing down our ideas helps us to clarify them. You might have to have several tries at formulating your hypotheses and/or objectives before you are satisfied with them.

Talk through your ideas with friends and relations. Brainstorming can be powerful in exploring topics and ways in which to conduct the enquiry. You will certainly find that your teacher will encourage you to engage in small group or whole class discussions, to explore your own ideas and to help colleagues to explore theirs. Mobilise your family to help you with your study, as well as a study partner or 'critical friend' (see later in the chapter).

(b) *How am I going to study this? - Choosing the methodology*

Once you have decided what you wish to study, you will be able to choose what is the most appropriate way to study it, that is, the overall design of the study, whether it is an observational study, or a survey, or experiment. You must also think about the kind of data you might gather and the best way to present and analyse your data. Remember that your criterion for success is to fulfil your 40 skills, so it may well be that, in order to cover all 40, you need to select an appropriate methodology that will fulfil the skills; for example, skills A2 and A3 which demonstrate an understanding of the nature of dependent and independent variables will most effectively be accomplished through a laboratory or controlled experiment. So it may be that the need to fulfil a criterion by use of a particular methodology will in fact determine your choice of topic. This 'working backwards' is quite usual, and can be very helpful in keeping you focused in your study.

(c) *Who am I going to study? - Considering the availability of resources*

You need to gear your field of enquiry to your own lifestyle and availability of resources. If you are studying aspects of the behaviour of nurses, or police, or teachers, or any other body of people, have you access to those people? If you want to investigate people's attitudes towards a particular topic, have you access to people with first-hand knowledge about that topic? It is pointless asking people to answer a questionnaire to find out their views on television soap operas if they don't watch television. These are all common sense points, but often, when we want to undertake a psychological investigation, we tend to get carried away with the possibilities and lose sight of the everyday practicalities. Good advice is - keep the project small, focused and on task: aim simply to fulfil the 40 skills.

(d)   What sort of evidence can I gather? How will I make sense of the evidence? - Organising the data

From the outset, aim to keep careful records. This means planning, and then keeping records to show how the planning is translated into action.

Plan the enquiry from the start. You need to decide on your data-gathering techniques. Are you going to administer questionnaires? If so, what kind will they be? Are you going to interview people? How? Where? How will you gather the raw data? How will you convert it? How will you draw up the tables to show these data and present them in graphic form? Do not make up your coursework as you go along. Plan the whole thing beforehand for successful implementation.

There are two very useful techniques here: heuristics (asking questions) and a SWOT analysis.

Heuristics

In planning your research, ask yourself the questions Who?, What?, Which?, When?, Where? You can also ask How? and Why?, although you might not be able to furnish any kind of answer for these last two in empirical research. Use the first five heuristics when you address every issue; for example, for your questionnaire, you might ask:

> Who will I ask?
> What will I ask them?
> When will I do this?
> Where will I conduct the exercise?
> Which questions will I ask?

You can apply the questions to any situation or aspect of the enquiry.

SWOT analysis

You can also apply a SWOT analysis to any situation or aspect of the enquiry. SWOT stands for Strengths, Weaknesses, Opportunities and Threats. So, again looking at issues to do with a questionnaire, consider:

Strengths - a questionnaire is a more efficient vehicle in this context than an interview.

Weaknesses - I shall have to make sure that the questions are quite specific, as the area that I am investigating is multi-faceted.

Opportunities - there might be an opportunity in this situation of discovering information that will throw light on a number of different aspects.

Threats - some of my participants might find the questionnaire threatening, so I must be sensitive in approaching them with the idea.

Do this kind of SWOT analysis for the major issues that you are addressing in formulating an action plan. Write it down in rough as part of your preparation. Ask your teacher to help you analyse (take apart) and synthesise (put together). Thinking things through beforehand is an essential part of working towards a successfully completed project.

2   Organise yourself

GCSE Psychology courses usually run for one or two years. One-year courses are becoming increasingly frequent, particularly in adult education environments. In fact, a one-year course means a 9-10 month course, from September to June. The written examination is taken in June. Coursework has to be with the moderator by 31st May of the year in which the written examination is to take place (unless it is carried forward in exceptional circumstances). This means that the Centre will need the coursework in at least by the middle, if not at the beginning, of May. Easter often intervenes here, so it is realistic to plan to have the coursework complete by the end of the Spring term, before Easter. This effectively gives six or seven months' study, often from scratch, before the completion of your coursework - not a particularly easy option, but perfectly realistic, if you plan your study effectively and systematically, and organise yourself appropriately. The following pointers should help.

(a)   Take yourself seriously as a student

Whether you are sixteen or sixty, you need to take your examination seriously. This does not mean that you have to make heavy weather of it. The examination is easily within your grasp if you study systematically, and life is too short to worry unnecessarily about examinations. However, if you have entered for the examination, then you owe it to yourself to organise your life in a way that will let you get a good grade.

Taking yourself seriously means letting people know that you are entered for an examination course, and asking them to recognise your rights as a learner. It also means getting the right tools for the job, practising your own study skills, and learning to access other resources and information databases for the information you require. Let's take these points in turn.

The right tools for the job

(i)   The right books

Your teacher will probably select or advise on your coursebooks. There are a number of good books on the market. S/he will probably choose one or two that cover the syllabus most comprehensively. Do not expect, however, that you will learn everything there is to know from the coursebooks. You need to be prepared to read much more widely. Your teacher might suggest that you purchase one or two supplementary books. This is always a useful investment. Coursebooks tend to say much the same thing, but in different ways, and the change of style and presentation can act as a powerful reinforcement.

Do use your library. If the books are not in stock, ask the library if they can get them for you. Many libraries operate an exchange system, and can arrange to get books in. If there is sufficient demand, they will buy in new books.

Do not limit your reading only to set or recommended books, though clearly this is a useful starting point. Read psychology texts first hand, if the subject matter interests you. Read newspapers and journals - keep a scrapbook or other archive of articles. Reference them in your coursework.

(ii)   *Develop an index system*

Develop some kind of indexing or referencing system. These can take different forms. Useful ways of keeping a check on what you have learnt would be to develop a card index system. You can buy card index boxes for about £3-5. A small box with torn up pieces of used A4 paper will do just as well. You would write the name of the psychologist on the card, and then a brief account of the work that s/he did. Instead of a card index, you might like to keep an alphabetical loose-leaf folder, or even a book whose pages you mark up alphabetically. A large telephone index or address book is quite useful here.

You could develop a cross-referencing system by writing down categories of psychological enquiry on a card, such as 'perception' or 'learning theories', and then writing in the names of the psychologists under these titles as you come across them. This kind of exercise is really helpful when it comes to revision time. Someone can pull out a card and test you on your subject knowledge, or you can carry your cards or book with you and revise at odd moments.

In developing your coursework, such a card indexing system is really useful also for gathering the data. For example, you could use this database for locating your own project within the wider literature, or draw examples from your database to support any conclusions you might come to in your project work.

(iii)   *The right equipment*

When you have finished writing up your project, you should submit it in a soft-back file, or even as loose leaves secured with treasury tags. **Do not** submit it in hardback folders or plastic pockets.

While you are preparing it, however, get yourself a proper file with dividers to keep your work organised. You will need separate sections for rough work, jottings, copies of questionnaires, record sheets, data analysis, graphical representations, and so on. Remember to submit graphics on graph paper, so you may need to purchase a small quantity of that, too.

(iv)   *A place to study*

If it is possible, arrange a place to study. It is important that your study station should be business-like, welcoming, and generally helpful to learning. You are going to spend about five hours a week on your psychology in general (this will vary according to how you are studying), of which about two hours will be spent each week on project work (not counting field work). Aim to organise your books and papers so that they are easily accessible. You need to spend the time you have available on your study, not hunting for a scrap of paper or a pen that might work. Organise and plan in advance, and your work should run smoothly and successfully.

(b) Organise your time

You are working to a very tight schedule in producing your coursework. If you are following a two-year course you can afford to be more relaxed. If you are following a one-year course, you have your work cut out.

Organise your time to maximise your chances of examination success, on a short, medium and long term basis.

Short term

Organise each day at the beginning of the day, or the evening before. If possible, work out a weekly schedule. Good time-management is the secret of success in many walks of life. Draw up a schedule for the day, breaking it up into blocks of an hour or, maximum, two hours. Concentration drops off after about an hour, so intersperse periods of study with periods of a different kind of activity. Here is an example of the kind of plan you might draw up.

Workplans for students in full time education

Workplan for a day in college	
9.00-10.10	lecture
10.15-10.45	break
10.45-11.45	lecture
11.45-12.45	lunch break
12.45- 1.30	quiet study
1.30- 2.30	lecture
2.30- 3.30	lecture
3.30- 4.00	tea break
4.00- 5.00	study
5.00- 5.30	go home
5.30- 6.00	watch television
6.00-7.30	break/tea
7.30-9.30	study

Workplan for a private study day	
9.00-10.15	study
10.15-10.45	coffee break
10.45-12.30	study
12.30- 1.15	lunch break
1.15- 2.00	study
2.00- 3.30	go for a walk
3.30- 5.00	study
5.00- 7.30	break
7.30- 9.30	study

Workplans for part-time students at work

Workplan for a workplace-based day	
9.00-12.30	office
12.30-1.30	lunch
	read 10 pages of psychology book
1.30-5.00	office
5.00-8.00	home/dinner/family
8.30-9.30	study

Workplan for a non-workplace-based day	
9.00-10.00	study
10.00-12.00	family/break
12.00-1.00	study
1.00 -2.00	family/lunch
2.00-3.30	study
3.30-7.30	family/break
7.30-8.30	study
8.30	family

These are ideas, not fixed plans. They are offered here to prompt you to think how you might organise your day, and to impress on you the value of time management by drawing up a plan in order to organise your time.

Aim to do most of your studying, if possible, when you know you are at your most effective. Some people are 'morning people', while others are 'night-owls'. You know yourself best, but do not cheat and say that you are a night-owl when really you know you don't want to get going first thing in the morning.

If you are working as well as studying, you will have to be strict with yourself and allocate certain times of the day or week for study periods. This calls also for the full co-operation of other family members (see below). But don't drive yourself to distraction. Leisure time is also a vital part of the learning process; you need quiet times and recreation to let the learnt material consolidate. You also need to live a normal life and pay attention to friends and family.

Do not do your assignments just before class. Get them done at leisure, so that you can actively study and reflect during assignment time, and use the time in class constructively for on-site learning.

Medium term

Organise each week on a regular basis. Make out a weekly schedule to fit study in with all the other demands, something like this:

For students in a school context

Your timetable may well be pre-arranged. It might look something like this example. If you work to a pre-arranged timetable, aim also to arrange your evening to fit in and balance study and leisure time (see below).

	Monday	Tuesday	Wednesday	Thursday	Friday
9.00-10.00	lesson	lesson	lesson	lesson	lesson
10.00-11.00	lesson	lesson	lesson	lesson	lesson
11.00-11.20			break		
11.20-12.30	lesson	lesson	lesson	lesson	lesson
12.30- 1.15			lunch		
1.15- 2.15	lesson	lesson	lesson	lesson	lesson
2.15- 3.30	lesson	lesson	lesson	lesson	lesson
end of school day					

For students in a college situation

You are in a more flexible situation than students in school, so the responsibility is more on you to organise your time. A notional weekly plan for you could look like the one on page 35:

Monday	Tuesday	Wednesday	Thursday	Friday
9.00-10.30 lecture	9.00-10.00 private study	9.00-10.30 lecture	9.00-10.30 lecture	9.00-10.00 private study
10.30-11.00 lecture	10.00-11.30 lecture	10.30-12.00 private study	10.45-1.00 lecture	10.00-12.00 lecture
11.00-12.00 lecture	11.30-12.30 lunch	12.00-1.00 lunch	1.00-2.00 lunch	12.00-12.30 tutorial
12.00-1.00 lunch	12.30-1.30 lecture	1.00-3.00 lecture	2.00-3.00 private study	12.30-1.00 go home
1.00-2.00 private study	1.30-1.45 break	3.00-3.30 go home	3.00-5.00 lecture	1.00-2.00 lunch
2.00-2.30 break	1.45-3.00 lecture	3.30-4.00 break	5.00-5.30 break	2.00-4.00 private study
2.30-3.30 lecture	3.00-4.00 private study	4.00-6.00 study	5.30-6.30 lecture	4.00-5.00 break
3.30-4.00 go home	4.00-5.00 lecture	6.00-7.00 tea	6.30-7.00 go home	5.00-6.00 study
4.00-5.00 break	5.00-5.30 go home	7.00 go out	7.00-8.00 tea	6.00 go out
5.00-6.00 study	5.30-7.00 break/tea		8.00-10.00 study	
6.00-7.00 tea	7.00-7.30 study			
7.00-8.30 television	7.30-10.30 television			
8.30-10.00 study				

You can arrange your weekend to suit your own purposes as proposed in the example on page 33.

Whatever your context, make sure you plan an evening for maximum effectiveness. An average evening might look something like this:

5.30	arrive home
6.00-6.30	TV/relax
6.30-7.00	tea
7.00-8.00	study
8.00-9.00	break/TV
9.00-10.00	study

Within this schedule, aim to vary the amount of time you spend on leisure and on study time, and also aim to vary the timings of those various activities. You need to spend time with family and friends, and also by yourself, as much as you need to spend time studying. It is a question of getting the right balance, making sure that you study effectively but not to the extent that you give up a pleasurable lifestyle for an unmitigated slog.

For part-time students already at work: you will need to spend at least five hours a week on psychology, if not more. There is no point in doing the course unless you can give the time. You need to ask yourself, 'What am I going to take out of my life that occupies 5-10 hours a week, in order to put psychology in?'

Long term

As well as weekly planners, make out a monthly timetable. Fit your study around commitments. Write in commitments and deadlines. Get a yearly planner, and put it prominently near your workstation, so that you can see at a glance what you have to do and when you have to do it. Use coloured pens to indicate different jobs. Use your imagination in how you can manage your own time effectively. If you are a full time student at school, this kind of forward planning is essential.

For students on one-year courses you need to recognise that you are working to a tight schedule, and work out schedules and action plans in the time available. It is usually easier to work out this kind of plan backwards, thinking of the final date for submission, and then fitting in deadlines.

Be very careful about meeting deadlines. Your teacher is also operating to strict deadlines. S/he has no control over submission dates, so you must co-operate here. Always allow yourself a little latitude in handing in work. Aim for an ideal deadline for yourself one week before the actual final date. If you meet it, you have a week of pressure-free time; if you don't you will still not be late.

For your coursework, planning is crucial. You need to draft everything first. You will probably have to do two or three drafts of everything before producing a fair copy. This drafting programme itself calls for time management. You need to construct a clear time-scale for creating, piloting and implementing questionnaires. If you are conducting a controlled experiment you need to arrange with your colleagues taking part when they will be free. You need to have all your equipment ready well in advance. Remember also that you might need to let colleagues know the results of your study: this is all part of good, ethical scientific practice.

Holidays

These are opportunities for intensive study and revision. How you organise your time depends on your desire to succeed, and also your other personal, family and business commitments. General advice is:

❏ Aim to balance study and leisure. Aim to designate at least 4 days a week as study days.

❏ Make a written plan and stick to it. Ask someone else to help you to stick to your good intentions.

❏ Aim to do your work in the morning. Those who say, 'I'll leave it till the afternoon' usually leave it altogether.

❏ Make out an 'objectives' list at the beginning of the holidays: '*By the end of the first two weeks, I will have revised chapters 1-15; by the end of the holidays I will have done the whole book.*'

❏ Make time to relax. Don't drive yourself into the ground. Holidays are a time for re-charging your batteries, and the energy you gather from conscious relaxation will later be invested in intensified study and should produce improved results.

Advice for people working independently

The rest of this chapter is aimed at mature students in adult education or independent study contexts. Students in schools and colleges may skip to the next chapter.

If you are working by yourself, or in an adult education environment, where you are studying perhaps one or two single subjects, you will be responsible for your own work organisation. You must organise yourself effectively. Your task is much more difficult than that of full-time students who have their studies organised for them to a greater or lesser degree. Try to work out an overall framework for yourself along these lines:

An example of an action plan

Here is a notional action plan for conducting coursework.

Tom Brown's Coursework

I am doing two projects. (I am doing only two because I am an adult student on a one-year programme. My son who is a student at school on a two-year programme is doing three projects.) My first project is a controlled experiment to test the effect of interference on memory. This will cover the skills in Domain A, as well as others. The second is a survey into people's attitudes towards cartoons on television. This will cover skills in Domain B, as well as other skills. My teacher has offered to make notes and exercises available to me for any skills which I might not have covered. Here is my action plan.

For Project 1 I shall conduct a laboratory experiment. In this experiment I shall ask ten friends and colleagues to assemble in a quiet place. Perhaps I shall invite them to my home. I shall ask them to watch attentively while I shuffle a pack of cards, and then place 15 cards face up on the table in front of them. I shall give them a minute to memorise the cards. Then I shall remove the cards and, after a short delay, give them one more minute to write down the cards they remember. I shall then record the scores.

A week later I shall ask the same group to do the same exercise again. This time, when I have given them one minute to memorise the cards and then proceed to remove them, I shall talk about the television programmes I watched the evening before. I shall also ask them questions about what they watched. This will provide the interference I need in accordance with my hypothesis. I shall then ask them to write down the cards they remember. I anticipate that the results on trial 2 will be lower than those on trial 1.

For Project 2 I shall conduct a survey into people's attitudes to watching cartoons on television. I shall prepare a questionnaire, which I will first pilot on six friends and colleagues, and then I shall administer the questionnaire to passers-by one morning in Poole town centre. I shall then organise and analyse the results at my leisure.

My action plan for conducting my coursework is this:

October-November: make myself familiar with research methods; read the appropriate chapters in my text books; borrow and read books from the library on research methods, compilation of questionnaires, analysing and interpreting data, presenting the results in graphic form. Note to myself: I do not need to read the books cover to cover - only select from them the information that I need.

November-December: rough out plan for overall projects. Research different kinds of design. Check with teachers and colleagues if my planned investigations are methodologically accurate. Think about questionnaire for Project 2.

December: Do a trial run of Project 1 on family and close friends. Test for any flaws in the design. Re-think any suspect aspects. Draft questionnaire for Project 2 and pilot on family and close friends, and perhaps students in psychology class.

Relax over Christmas holiday. Do some general psychology reading.

January: Do first run of experiment in week 3. Do second run of experiment in week 4. Write up method. Collate and analyse results. Review and refine questionnaire. Ask teacher for notes and exercises on specific skills not yet covered.

February: write up Project 1. Choose a fine day to run questionnaire in Poole town centre. Also ask fellow students to complete questionnaire. Collate and analyse all results. Write up Project 2. Do teacher-generated exercise for any skills not yet covered.

February-March: Write up all coursework. Submit by end of March.

As already noted, this schedule is one of many. The idea of drawing up an action plan, however, is a great way to focus the mind for action. Before you begin your coursework, then, please draw up a monthly calendar, and fill in on the left hand side what your proposed action plan is, and then fill in what you achieve on the right hand side as you go. This will keep you on line for completing your coursework on time, if not a little in advance.

Planning is vital. Time spent on planning is time well invested.

Organise your family

... and your friends, and any other people who are close to you. Let them know that you are taking your studies seriously, and make it clear that you expect them to respect your wishes.

Organise the family. They have to help you, not hinder you. Get your husband or wife or partner to do at least one of the household tasks that you usually do, so that you gain a little more time. Ask the children to help you.

Get the family to help you to study. They are your first allies when you need to find research participants. Get them to help you to formulate your questionnaires, or come up with brilliant ideas for experiments. Ask them to check your calculations, or to dream up different ways of presenting the data. Your family are your closest supporters.

Organise your friends and colleagues. Ask them to be participants in your experiments, to fill in questionnaires or record opinion. A study evening could turn into a social evening. At the same time, make sure they respect you and your work. If Wednesday is your study evening, they should not tempt you out. If they care about you, they care about your success.

Get your family and friends to listen to you talk about psychology. Give them your 5x3 reference cards, and get them to test you.

Find a critical friend or study partner. This person is often to be found in your psychology class, but may also be drawn from your circle of family and friends. Get that person to listen to you carefully and sympathetically, but also critically. You do not need a supporter to be so supportive that they agree with everything you say. You need criticism to move your thinking forward, but it needs to be positive criticism of the kind, 'Yes, but have you thought about ... ?' Critical friends are wonderful allies.

What to do with your teacher

You might be a student in an organised learning environment, such as in a school, college, or adult and continuing education centre. You could also be working on a self-study or distance-learning basis. Whatever your learning context is, you need to use your teacher sensitively and effectively as one of your most able and accessible resources.

Teachers are people first, teachers second. They are real people who are competent but who do not know all the answers, who also sometimes have problems getting themselves organised, and who have to accept that they will be held personally responsible for the whole of psychological enquiry. By and large, teachers are well-meaning, caring, and reasonably efficient, and they are wonderfully grateful to you when you attempt to meet them on an equal footing, acknowledging that they are nice, ordinary human beings, just like you.

Do ask and expect your teachers to give you guidance. If you don't understand a point, ask them to explain it again. If they get stuck, respect this and ask them perhaps if they can give you the necessary information next time you meet. **Do not** aim to score points. Regard your course as a shared, negotiated learning experience, both for you and your teachers. It really is!

Do expect your teachers to check your work carefully and regularly. They might negotiate a marking schedule with you. If they set deadlines for submission of work, please respect the deadlines and meet them. You would expect your teachers to meet your agreed terms. This is a partnership, and you must all work together. **Do not** get cross if teachers are late in their marking. You might be late one day, too. Nobody is perfect.

Do choose your time to speak to teachers. Often, people think that they will take just a few minutes after class to check on something. If five people think the same thing, the strategy will not be very effective. Ask teachers if you can discuss something during class time. Never be anxious about negotiating the learning strategy. This is what effective management is all about. Spontaneous chats are not the most useful learning strategy; planned inputs and exchanges are much more productive.

And finally ...

Believe in yourself

At the end of the day, your most important resource is yourself. Believe in yourself, quietly, confidently and without arrogance. You have a right to be here. You have a right to study, to exercise your intellect, to think for yourself. You are a unique person with a unique contribution to make. Here is an opportunity. Life is a continuous learning process. This course is one chance to gain formal accreditation for that learning. Take the chance and use it. It might not be there again.

5 PLANNING YOUR RESEARCH PROJECT: SCIENTIFIC CONSIDERATIONS

In Chapter Four we looked at the four questions we need to ask in planning a scientific investigation. They are:

1 What aspect am I going to study?
2 How am I going to study it?
3 Who am I going to study?
4 What kind of evidence can I gather? How can I evaluate it?

This chapter now focuses on the scientific considerations, which are interrelated with the practical considerations already discussed.

1 What aspect am I going to study?

In empirical psychological research, the idea is that you are going to study aspects of human or non-human animal behaviour, and try to come to some understanding of why people and animals act as they do. If your aim is to stop at the level of observation and description, you would decide to conduct an observational study, where you note what is going on, and count heads or events.

The way in which you can infer reasons for why people or animals act as they do - cause and effect - is to study the variables in the situation. Strictly speaking, variables do not necessarily demonstrate a cause-and-effect relationship (you will look at this in your 'A' and higher level studies), but for the time being this is a useful starting point.

The variables you need to consider are dependent, independent, and extraneous variables.

Dependent and independent variables

Let's take the example on page 38. Remember that Tom Brown was aiming to test out his hypothesis that there was, in this case, a causal relationship between the number of cards that his subjects remembered and the degree of interference. He reckoned that no interference, or at least minimal interference, would provide a better context for them to remember the cards. If he introduced interference, he reasoned, that would interfere with the memory task and they would remember fewer cards.

In this example, the independent variable was the interference, or degree of interference. That was the aspect of the situation that he was changing, to test out and see whether it affected the situation. He was manipulating the independent variable (cause) to see if it had any influence on the outcome (effect) - otherwise known as the dependent variable: i.e., number of cards remembered.

Here is another example. Imagine that you want to find out if there really is a relationship between the amount of praise you receive and the degree of your success in performing a particular task. Imagine that you receive praise if you perform the task correctly. This increases your motivation because of your desire for praise, such that your performance improves dramatically. You could say that your performance (the DV) depended on the amount of praise you received (the IV). You can say that the dependent variable **depends on** the independent variable.

Can you identify the dependent variable (DV) and the independent variable (IV) in the following examples?

(1) Effect of an audience on people's performance;
(2) Effect of category headings on recall of a list of words;
(3) Effect of fin angles on the apparent extent of the Müller-Lyer illusion.

In (1), whether or not an audience is present will influence performance. The IV is the presence or absence of the audience, and the DV is performance.

In (2), success in recalling a list of words may be assisted by category headings; category headings are the IV and success in recall is the DV.

In (3), the extent of the Müller-Lyer illusion depends on the size of fin angles; the DV, extent of the illusion, depends on the IV, size of fin angles.

You can see that these three examples proceed from a common-sense basis. They are not being scientifically tested out here. There is no way that you can demonstrate that the DV actually does depend on the IV: that there is a relationship between audience presence and people's behaviour, between recall and category headings, or between fin angles and extent of Müller-Lyer illusion. These are all hunches, grounded in common sense and previous experience of the world (induction). If you wanted to produce evidence that there actually did appear to be a demonstrable connection, you would have to set about devising an experiment to test out those hunches in a much more controlled and scientific way (deduction). Then you would aim to test out the IV and DV, and evaluate them and their relationship in some way. There are a number of ways to carry out this evaluation, and, in empirical experiments, the most common way is to measure them - that is, give them a numerical value, and compare the numerical results. So, in (1), you could arrange for someone to perform a particular task with an audience present, and somehow record the performer's scores; and then ask another person to perform the same task without an audience, and then record those scores: and then you would compare the two sets of scores.

Now try to plan a test situation for the other two examples.

Extraneous variables

There are variables other than the independent and dependent variables. Two of these are known as confounding variables and extraneous variables. These terms are often interchanged, though technically there are differences. For our purposes, we shall lump both kinds together and call them extraneous variables.

Extraneous variables may be seen as those that cloud the issue. To go back to the example of amount of praise you receive and performance success - who is to say what else is motivating you to succeed? You might be a highly competitive person with an insatiable desire to succeed. You might want to live up to your sister's high academic standard. You might be naturally bright in that performance area. All these aspects could have an effect on the outcome. In order to test out the relationship between the praise and degree of success, you would have to screen out or otherwise control other extraneous variables, which is a very difficult thing to do and requires rigorous procedures.

In your coursework, Skill A5, you will need to suggest measures for controlling extraneous variables. This means that you will need to identify them, and then give clear explanations as to how you will control them - that is, try to make sure that they do not interfere with the assumed cause and effect relationship between the IV and the DV. You are trying to demonstrate that the IV influences the DV, so you have to ensure that you have kept the IV uncontaminated. When you come to writing up the report, it will not be sufficient to say, 'I controlled the extraneous variables.' You have to say quite clearly what you did so that the extraneous variables really did have minimal influence on the dependent variable.

In each of the following examples, identify which are the independent variables, the dependent variables, and any extraneous variables you might encounter. Say quite clearly how you would control the extraneous variables so that they had minimal influence on the outcome (the dependent variable). The answers are at the end of the chapter.

> (1) My sister claims that the colour of her hair is the important factor in how many boys ask her to dance at the disco.
>
> (2) I think I remember more of my psychology reading if I make notes as I go along.
>
> (3) I seem to remember more if I use green ink than if I use blue ink. I wonder why?
>
> (4) I want to see if reducing the amount of my son's television viewing will have any effect on the quality of his homework.

EXERCISE

2   How am I going to study it?

Here we are addressing issues of research design and methodology. The design refers to the overall structure of the study; the methodology is, broadly speaking, the way in which we are going to study those aspects we have identified. Different purposes require different methodologies: demonstrating causal relationships means doing an experiment or investigation; assessing people and events means doing an observational study; gathering opinion means doing a survey.

A note on 'method' and 'methodology'

Most researchers make a difference between the use of the words 'method' and 'methodology' (but not everyone applies the difference consistently). The difference lies, roughly speaking, in that 'method' is used to describe the steps you took in carrying out a specific task: compare, for example, when you are baking a cake, that there is a method - that is, a predetermined sequence of steps. You don't bake the ingredients before you have mixed them. Nor do you wash the car by rinsing first and then applying the shampoo. There is not such a clear method in doing the gardening, however, where you might do whatever job took your fancy first.

The idea of methodology embraces a wider understanding of how and why a specific method is adopted, and so has a much wider application. For purposes of GCSE work, try to use the word 'method' in terms of an action-step sequence, and the word 'methodology' to talk about the wider aspects of understanding the whole procedural form and its implications.

Experimental research design

Here is some more confusing language! The word 'design' may be used to refer to the whole structure of the enquiry - that is, the different aspects and sections involved, such as hypothesis formulation, procedure, data gathering and analysis, and so on. It may also be used in a more specific sense with reference to experimental research, where the researcher manipulates the variables in an attempt to control the outcomes. This is the aspect that we are addressing in this section.

In a moment we shall see that there are three kinds of experimental design you need to be familiar with in order to fulfil skill A6. They are repeated measures design, independent samples design and matched pairs design.

To go back a step, however, we need to appreciate that, in psychology, there are essentially two general frameworks, termed related and unrelated designs. In related designs, we ask the same group of people to do the same task under different conditions, such as remember cards with no interference (Condition A) and then remember cards with interference (Condition B). So:

Group 1	
Condition A	Condition B
without interference	with interference

In unrelated designs, we ask different people to do the same task under different conditions:

Group 1	Group 2
Condition A	Condition B
without interference	with interference

In related designs, the outcome in Condition A is related to the outcome in Condition B. In unrelated designs, the outcomes of the experiment are not related, since the groups themselves are not related.

Now, to be more specific:

In related designs, we have repeated measures design and matched pairs design; in unrelated designs we have single subject and independent samples. Coolican (1992) offers the following diagram

Design	In each condition	
	Same subject	**Different subject**
Related	Repeated measures	Matched pairs
Unrelated	Single subject	Independent samples

Repeated measures design

This is in the category of related designs, and it really does not matter at GCSE whether you use the terms 'repeated measures design' or 'related measures design'. The most important thing is that you know what it means and can use it.

Repeated measures design means that the same group does the same task under different conditions. In the card-memory experiment above, the same group would perform Task A (no interference) and Task B (with interference). You would then record their group scores as your data, and analyse it in terms of how each condition affected memory - that is, is memory improved by interference or by no interference?

Order effects

The problems with repeated measures design are those of order, practice and fatigue effects. These are the kinds of extraneous variables you need to take into account and control. According to the working hypothesis that 'interference is detrimental to memory' you might expect your participants' scores to drop significantly on Task B - remembering the cards while dealing with the alien aspect of interference. The result might not be like that, though. Some people might have developed a system to help them remember: for example, mentally organise all the cards into suits, or arrange them, from high to low numbers, and so on. This is known as the practice effect. Another aspect of the practice effect is that the participants might be used to the whole idea of being participants in an experiment by now and they might not be so on edge second time round. Also, they might have become bored, or tired, or got cramp - in which case, this is known as fatigue effect.

The method of combating order effects that you need to be familiar with is known as counterbalancing. This is where you split the group into two halves, now Groups 1^1 and 1^2, present Condition A to Group 1^1 first, and Condition B to Group 1^2 first. You then reverse the procedure. So:

	Group 1^1	Group 1^2
Condition	A	B
	B	A

Note - this has **not** now become an independent samples design (see below). It is still the same group, but operating in a different order solely for purposes of combating order effects. Counterbalancing is used in repeated measures designs.

Independent samples design

It does not matter at GCSE whether you use the terms 'independent samples design' or 'unrelated measures design'.

In an independent samples design, we have two groups of people doing the same task but under separate conditions: that is, either Condition A (without interference), or Condition B (with interference) (or with Conditions C,D,E, ...; such as with lengthy interference: the list of variations on a theme is substantial. At GCSE we'll stick with only two examples of different Conditions.) We then take the scores of Group 1 and Group 2 and compare them to try to see if Condition A or Condition B was more effective in helping them in their task. Depending on the scores, we could say that we had demonstrated a relationship between the variables as our hypothesis indicated (remember, you can't ever prove anything, so avoid the word 'prove'; use 'test' or 'indicate' or 'demonstrate' or other similar term).

Individual (subject) variables

If order effects are the problematic extraneous variables in repeated measures design, individual variables are the problem in independent samples design. The 'individuals' in the term are the people involved in the experiment, the people we are observing. (Until recently the conventional term was 'subject variables', but remember that we are systematically moving away from this usage.) Individual variables are all those things that are unique to the person, such as age, gender, culture, history, family relationships. These are also called 'individual differences'. Also peculiar to those individuals are contextual or environmental issues, such as how they are feeling, whether they are paying attention or not, if they have done something like this before. These differences are very difficult to eliminate, if not impossible: but it is possible to introduce various screening or pre-test measures to ensure that the individuals in both groups are reasonably similar. (Note: when you come to post-GCSE work, you will be encouraged to critique ideas, such as whether it actually is possible to treat people in the same way as plants or other inert, unthinking material. At GCSE level, however, we assume that it is.)

Implications for coursework

Skills A6 and A7 ask you to select an appropriate experimental design and justify your choice. In order to gain a mark you must say why you chose as you did. It is not enough to say, 'I chose a related measures design.' You need to go on to explain: for example, '... *because I wished to test the reactions of the same people under different experimental conditions.*'

Matched pairs design

In experiments where we need to ensure that members from two groups are as alike as possible, we go for a matched pairs design. Each individual in Group 1 is matched with a partner in Group 2, in terms of age, gender, physical build, and so on. It is, of course, quite impossible to ensure a perfect match, even with monozygotic (identical) twins. Matched pairs design is part of the related category, because the results on Task A have a direct bearing on Task B. They are related.

3   Who am I going to study?

In deciding on who you are going to observe and study you are considering which samples and groups you will choose and the methods you will employ to choose them.

Populations, samples and groups

A population is just that: the total population - all the people or things that own the certain characteristic you are interested in studying. A population can refer to things other than people: all the flowers in your garden, for example, or all the books about methods of enquiry. The idea of a population is that it refers to the whole lot that has the characteristic you are interested in. If you wanted to study that thing in detail, ideally you would investigate each and every member of that particular population. For example, if you wanted to study the habits of students in further or adult education, you would have to study them all. Clearly this is not possible, as there must be thousands, if not millions, of such people. The recourse then is to select a sample that is representative of the population. In this case, you would choose a number from further or adult education. You would reason that such a sample would behave in a way that would also be representative of the population, so you would be able to generalise from the sample and formulate general wide-ranging laws and principles.

There are a number of ways of sampling that are appropriate for GCSE psychological enquiry.

Random sampling

Technically, random sampling is a highly sophisticated process using lists of randomly-generated numbers. For our purposes, however, we can simply pick names out of a hat, or use a pin to select a name from a list, or throw dice. Everyone whose name appeared on a list would (theoretically) stand the same chance of being selected.

Opportunity sampling

This is the name given to the process by which we select anyone who happens to be available at the time. We as researchers are opportunists. We use whatever material we can have access to. Most GCSE candidates employ opportunity sampling, since they have not the time nor resources to go for another form which involves more time.

Quota sampling

In this kind of sampling we decide on the various groups we are going to study - nurses, police, students. We then decide the number of participants we need for our sample - say 10 of each of the groups. We invite 10 nurses to take part in our experiment. Once we have our quota of 10, we then do not invite any more. We do the same for any other groups whom we wish to be involved in the study.

Stratified sampling

Remember that a sample needs to be representative of the whole population. Say we wanted to gather opinion from certain identified groups within our population - if we wanted to do a survey of the college but decided to focus on students doing (a) business studies; (b) arts; (c) social care; and (d) engineering. Or say we wanted to do a survey about child welfare and we decided to gather opinion from (a) doctors; (b) welfare agencies; (c) health visitors; (d) parents. We could represent our population, containing those groups of people we are particularly interested in as all the (a)s, (b)s, (c)s and (d)s:

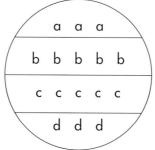

This is the whole population divided into strata (note: we say, 'one stratum' but 'two strata'). But, as we noted before, we cannot reach the total population, so we have to focus on a much smaller sample. In this case, the sample groups still have to be representative, as they are in the population, and be in the same proportion:

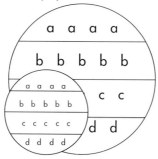

Cluster sampling

Say you wanted to gather opinion from people in a school of a particular age group, say Year 9. Instead of random sampling from the whole year group, which could be disruptive to all of the classes in the year group, you could choose a single class - that is, people who have come together as a group for a different reason.

Self-selected sampling

Participants in self-selected samples volunteer themselves. Suppose you are observing a phenomenon or event, such as people coming out of a cinema, and you ask people their opinions or involve them in some way. If they agree to be involved they may be seen as opting to be part of your sample by selecting themselves. Remember - they **elect** to be **selected**.

Size of sample

Many students ask about an ideal size for a sample group. This is a matter mainly of common sense. If it is too small (say 5), you will not get a representative sample, and your results will lead to a distorted generalisation. If the sample is too big (say 100), you will spend many laborious hours trying to make sense of all the data you gather.

A common sense response would be 10-20. You are at liberty to go above 20 if you have time and resources to gather and analyse the data. Anything below 10 may well not produce evidence that will act as generalisable material.

Subject groups

There are two types of groups to which we allocate people in experimental psychology. They are experimental groups, and control groups.

Experimental groups

This is the group of people who are involved in varied manipulated conditions. If we wanted to explore the effect of watching violence on television on the behaviour of children, as Bandura did, we would select a group of children to watch violent programmes as part of their viewing over time, and then we would observe any emergent violent trends, say, in their play. We might conclude that the television violence had a bearing on real life behaviour. However, this is **NOT** an experiment which you should attempt, for ethical reasons.

Control groups

To make sure that any resultant increase in violent behaviour was not because of chance, we would also have a control group who had not consciously been exposed to violence on television, but had watched something else. We would then be able to compare and contrast the behaviour of the control group with that of the experimental group, thinking that there would be a significant change in the behaviour of the experimental group, such that we could say that the emerging emphasis on violent behaviour (the DV) was directly as a result of the experimental condition of watching violence on television (the IV).

In coursework it is not always necessary to have a control group. The choice of related or unrelated measures designs is often enough.

4   What kind of evidence can I gather? How can I evaluate it?

In attempting to address these questions, we focus on two major aspects of scientific enquiry: validity and reliability.

Validity

A test or result is valid if it does what it sets out to do. If you claim that new Washo washing powder really does get whites even whiter, but it does not in fact produce any more startling results than it did before, then your claim is invalid. If you run a test to see if people's perception of familiar words is faster than their perception of unfamiliar words, and then you don't use any unfamiliar words in the test, the test itself would be invalid. It would not be testing or demonstrating a result in the area it said it was. Think of the idea of invalid entry to an event; or of a ticket that has expired and is now invalid. To enter that place or to use the ticket would not be legitimate. The same principle applies to tests and results: for them to be valid they must be right for the job, and they must be backed up with clear, unambiguous evidence.

1	2	3
4	5 **3**	6
7	8	9

Here is an example of an invalid test. Suppose you were presented with this puzzle. You are given this diagram, which is meant to be a test of numerical ability, and then you are asked certain questions to help you find the numbers for you to fill in the other squares. Question 1 is, 'What is the sum of 2 + 5?' No problem here: the answer is 7. Question 2 is, 'What was the number of a film starring Dustin Hoffman?' The answer is '10'. However, this last question is inappropriate, and makes the test invalid; it is not testing numerical ability, but is testing knowledge of film titles. Guard against such phenomena when you are constructing your own tests. Always think, does the test do what is says it is going to do?

Reliability

We say of a person, or a clock, or the weather: 'It's reliable' or 'It's unreliable'. That means that we can depend on it to act in much the same way that it has always done and we have grown to expect. For John to arrive late after two years of punctuality would be exceptional; we would say it is out of character. For Susie to arrive sometimes on time and sometimes late would be nothing unusual. She is generally unreliable.

In conducting experiments, reliability is an essential ingredient. The test or result is said to be reliable if the test or result of another identical experiment was the same or nearly the same. We say a clock is reliable if it tells the same time on two or more consecutive days. We say a test is reliable if it produces the same result on two or more occasions. For people to take the results of experiments seriously and to regard them as having generalisability potential, the experiment must be repeated many times with the same or nearly the same result.

This is the issue of replicability. If an experiment may be replicated - duplicated - to produce a similar result, it may be said to be a good, reliable experiment. This has implications for writing up coursework. When you come to writing up, always bear the criterion of replicability in mind. If I were to read what you have written, would I be able to reproduce your action steps and your procedures? Would I be able to understand the thinking you engaged in, in order to do things the way that you did? Would I get more or less the same results? You need to write and present your report in such a way that I will have no problems in replicating it.

Inter-observer reliability

A test is called reliable if it produces much the same result every time. Inter-observer reliability is when the persons observing the events agree that they are observing and perceiving the same things. If I say the boy is wearing a red jumper and you say it is blue, clearly we have no inter-observer reliability. When we are working with others to try to understand a situation we are watching, it is essential to aim for inter-observer reliability. We can do this by organising a pre-test trial run, where we would identify certain aspects of what we are observing and share our observations. If, in the red/blue jumper situation, I turned out to be visually insensitive to certain colours, I would disqualify myself, and someone else would take my place. Pre-test discussion is vital here, to make sure that observers are on the same wavelength, and that they are agreeing criteria and strategies.

Inter-scorer reliability

Similarly, scorers need to agree their criteria and strategies for scoring. In the marking of GCSE coursework where the teacher is the first line marker, groups of teachers meet to go through marking exercises - standardisation - so that they agree what they are doing and iron out any difficulties. Radical points of view have to be modified or somehow accommodated. Marking schemes have to be universally agreed and acted upon. It is no use candidates undertaking an examination if they cannot be assured of inter-scorer or inter-examiner reliability.

This concludes the most pressing practical and scientific considerations in planning your coursework. In chapter 6 we turn to various types of investigations you can do, when some of these considerations will begin to fall into place.

Answers to questions on page 44:

(1) IV is colour of her hair; DV is number of boys who ask her to dance. Extraneous variables could be: her general appearance on the night; how many other partners are available to dance; if she has a reputation for being a good dancer.

(2) IV is note-taking; DV is amount of psychology reading remembered. Extraneous variables could be: my level of motivation to remember; how interesting the reading material is; my memory ability in general.

(3) IV is colour of ink; DV is amount of material I remember. Extraneous variables could be: my level of attention; how often I read the material to be remembered; how familiar the material already is.

(4) IV is amount of television viewing: DV is quality of homework. Extraneous variables could be: level of his motivation; other distracting factors; his level of alertness; any rewards you might have offered if he is successful.

Reference

Coolican, H. (1992), *Research Methods and Statistics in Psychology*; Hodder and Stoughton.

PART 3
IMPLEMENTATION

This part looks as procedure, and offers a 'how to do it' guide for conducting an enquiry and for gathering documentary evidence. Documentary evidence is taken to mean any way in which we can keep a retrievable record, so this includes use of audiovisual media. You are offered advice on the construction and implementation of record sheets, questionnaires, interviews and keeping diaries and logs. These record sheets are used in first-hand experience of gathering the raw data. In Part Four we shall look at how to interpret and present the data that our documentary evidence provides, in organising the raw data into a comprehensible form.

Chapter 6 explains the different types of investigation you can undertake · experiments and investigations, observations, surveys and case studies. It gives step-by-step guidance on how to do them.

Chapter 7 shows you how to draw up record sheets for gathering data.

Chapter 8 gives practical advice on devising and administering questionnaires and attitude scales.

Chapter 9 tells you how to conduct interviews.

Chapter 10 advises you on keeping diaries.

⑥ TYPES OF INVESTIGATION

In this chapter we want to outline the main types of investigation and to indicate how you might set about doing them. The types of investigation we shall consider are:

    experiments and investigations (laboratory and field)
    observations
    interviews and surveys
    case studies

Interviews and case studies are not yet prominent in GCSE psychology coursework, but it is as well that you know what they are about, so they are included here.

Experiments and investigations

A real experiment is an enquiry in which the experimenter manipulates the independent variable. The experiment may be conducted in the laboratory or in the field, but the experimenter must be able to have manipulated the IV for it to be called an experiment. An investigation which is not an experiment may be an enquiry in which there is a clearly identified IV and DV, but the experimenter does not, or is not able to, control and manipulate the IV.

An example of an experiment is this:

Imagine that you want to test the effects of perceptual set on perception. Your hypothesis is that perceptual set will influence perception of an ambiguous figure. You decide to use Leeper's lady in your enquiry. The assumption you hold is that, if participants have been exposed to pictures of young ladies, they will perceive Leeper's young lady first. If they have been exposed to pictures of older ladies, they will perceive Leeper's older lady first.

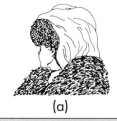
(a)

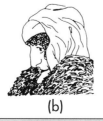
(b)

(c)

You choose two groups, Group 1 and Group 2, each consisting of 10 people. You show each member of Group 1 a sequence of 20 pictures of young ladies, some placed in the picture in the same pose as Leeper's young lady. You then show them Leeper's ambiguous lady, and test their perception by asking them to say what they see in the picture. You then note their response. You do exactly the same for Group 2, only showing them a sequence of 20 pictures of older ladies. (Note that this is an independent samples design.) You then count the number of responses, enter the results in a contingency

	Group 1	Group 2
Young lady	16	2
Old lady	4	18

table and draw some conclusions about the relationship between the DV and the IV. In this experiment you have controlled the IV - that is, the kind of stimulus, whether the young lady or the older lady. The results of the enquiry appear to have depended on your manipulation of this IV.

In your coursework you must do an experiment to gain many of the skills in Domain A. It is possible to cover all the other skills by not doing an experiment. It is wise to do a controlled experiment to make sure that you cover everything, certainly in Domain A.

Investigations

Investigations are enquiries that are similar to experiments but they are different in that the researcher does not manipulate the IV. It is usually field investigation that comes into this category, though laboratory studies may do so as well.

An example of a laboratory investigation is this: you want to see whether playing loud music while they are doing their homework interferes with your children's level of concentration. Your home now becomes the laboratory. You could conceivably set up a repeated measures design experiment, where you played loud music on Tuesday, while the children were studying (Condition A), and then had silence on Thursday (Condition B). The ethics of the study might be questionable, however. Instead, you could check the results of homework which is done while, from their choice, the children have been playing loud music; then perhaps you insist on a period of several evenings of calm (to give them time to accommodate to the novelty - they might say this was unethical!) and check the results of homework done under these conditions. You have still manipulated the IV here, but you have capitalised on an already existing situation and compared behaviours over time. (There would be a good argument here to change the whole focus of the study and turn it into a case study - see below).

Another example, this time of a field investigation, is this: You want to find out if children with siblings tend to be more sociable than children without siblings. The IV here is whether the child is an only child or one among others. Clearly you cannot control this IV. You could watch children at play, having previous knowledge who is and is not an only child, and note their sociability levels. You could do this in the field (playgrounds) or in the laboratory (a playgroup in a neighbour's house). However, you could not interfere with the situation in terms of controlling the IV, so any results or conclusions you might draw could not be directly attributed to the IV - that is, whether or not they are only children. If you wanted to extend this study to become an experiment, then you could **select** only children and children with siblings, allocate them to distinct groups, and test their sociability, either in the field or in the laboratory (unrelated measures design). This experimental focus then shows that you have deliberately controlled the IV and any conclusion you draw will bring out the inferred connection between IV (status of child) and DV (degree of sociability).

Laboratory conditions

Your laboratory may be anywhere, provided the context is one in which you are able to manipulate the IV. You don't have to, as in the example above, but you have the option. It may be in your home, your workplace, outdoors, a classroom situation. You may bring people into the laboratory and simply observe them, or you may allocate them to groups or activities as you manipulate the IV. The main idea of laboratory conditions is that you tend to be in direct control of organising your options and your participants - the action comes to you.

Field conditions

In this case, you go to the action. Field studies are studies which are conducted in naturalistic settings, such as an airport, a waiting room, an office, a public place. These field conditions often make it difficult for the researcher to manipulate the IV. Usually what you do is observe, note your observations, and draw conclusions from an analysis of your data. You may draw out general conclusions, but you may not strictly speaking assume a cause-and-effect relationship between the IV and DV if you have not manipulated the IV and shown that the IV has any observable bearing on the DV. To do this, you would have to choose a sample group, and set up some kind of controlled experiment with them, to test in detail the kinds of ideas you hold about the wider field experience.

Problems

There are some problems associated with experiments and investigations. They fall into several categories, two of which are discussed here: assumptions about the nature of human relationships; and problems of researcher bias.

Assumptions about the nature of human relationships

Human relationships are often power relationships with one party being the 'knower' and the other party being the 'trainee'. In a lot of empirical psychological research, the experimenter is regarded as a 'knower', and does research on other people. The researcher often becomes the 'outsider' researcher doing research on 'insiders'.

In democratic societies, large or small (and this includes a research society, including classroom situations) there are good arguments why this power relationship may be judged unfair. People should not be other people's objects, to be controlled and manipulated. People should have equal rights and entitlements. Some psychologists argue that psychological research should be about understanding the reasons which drive us so that we can improve our understanding and our social situation, and not primarily to control and predict. From a humanistic point of view, we are here to work together to improve the quality of life.

Problems of researcher bias

Empirical researchers acknowledge that there are problems of researcher bias, because researchers bring their individual differences with them to the research. These individual differences may cause certain effects, such as a 'loose procedure effect', when the procedure is not clearly reported and therefore cannot be easily replicated. Other problems are lack of inter-researcher reliability, where the results of two or more researchers may not agree; and 'personal attribute' effect, when, say, a participant is attracted to the researcher and his or her performance varies accordingly. Some people argue that these problems may be overcome by subjecting researchers to screening procedures or other exercises aimed at standardising their procedures and attitudes; but it is questionable whether such standardisation is possible or desirable among people.

Conducting experiments and investigations

HOW TO DO . . .

Here is a general action plan for conducting experiments and investigations.

1. Decide on what you want to find out. You must identify an area of study that compares or contrasts the behaviour of two groups (or more, but not for GCSE) under different conditions (at GCSE, only Condition A and Condition B - not more).

2. Decide on a working hypothesis about how people are affected by the different conditions. For example:

    How cold a room is will influence the amount of clothing that people wear.
    How bright a room is will influence how well people perceive objects.
    How familiar a word is will influence how well people remember it.

    Aim to establish a cause and effect relationship between the conditions and their influence on people. Turn the working hypothesis into a clearly formulated statement:

    'Temperature influences the amount of clothing people wear.'
    'Degree of brightness improves people's perception.'
    'Words which are familiar will be better remembered than words which are unfamiliar.'

3. Select your sample. Use any of the sampling methods discussed in chapter 5. Consider the suitability of participants, and also their availability.

4. Decide which experimental design to use. Will you use repeated measures, independent samples, or matched pairs design? Think about variables and how to control them. Think about order, practice and fatigue effects, and how to control them - counterbalancing, perhaps.

5. Decide on type of record sheet needed. Use any of the ideas given in chapter 7 or in chapter 11, or, better, create your own.

6. Pilot the study. Try it out on a few friends.

7. Re-think and change any aspects that are not well formulated, or that might lead to inappropriate results. Keep the pilot work.

8. Make a time for the experiment or investigation. Inform your participants. Ask them to be punctual if you are all meeting in one place.

9. Conduct the experiment or investigation at the designated time and place. Keep a record of your participants' responses, using your record sheet.

10. De-brief your participants. Thank them and explain to them what the purpose of the study was. Explain how important their involvement was.

11. Consider and organise the results on the record sheets. Draw up a table (chapter 11) to show the results, particularly how the different groups reacted under different conditions.

12. Perform calculations on the data (for GCSE find two out of the percentage, mean, median, ratio or range). Compare the results of the two groups and see if the results actually do bear out your initial hypothesis - or were the results due to chance?

13. Consider you findings. Will you keep your hypothesis or reject it? Does the previous literature have any bearing on your study? Can your study contribute to the literature? Were there any weaknesses in your overall design that produced a peculiar result?

14. Write the report.

Observations

The word 'observation' may be used in two ways in psychological research: (1) referring to the overall design: an observational study rather than an experimental study; (2) referring to the technique - observation rather than questioning, for example.

Observation as a technique is the basis of most scientific investigation. We watch reality, and we make intelligent guesses about how and why it works as it does. We then bring in other techniques, such as questioning, controlling and manipulating, to see if we can understand things better by trying to isolate and examine their component parts (analysis), and draw a meaningful relationship between those parts (synthesis).

Observational studies focus on trying to describe a situation as it is. The weakness in this kind of study, from an empirical point of view, is that the factors being observed cannot be interfered with and therefore no generalisation may be made about the relationship between the variables, and no cause and effect relationship can be demonstrated. Its strength lies in the fact that the behaviour being observed is free and unconstrained.

Participant and non-participant observation

The researcher-observer may either be part of the action (participant) or excluded from the action (non-participant), or enjoy varying degrees of participation. Certain aspects of either approach need to be taken into account when considering the findings of the observation. In participant observation, if the members of the group to be studied know what the observer's role is, they may modify their behaviour, perhaps to fall in with what they see as the observer's expectations, or to protect themselves from the observer, and so on. If observers do not disclose the true purpose of their study, they may well be guilty of deception and unethical behaviour. If they do disclose the true nature of their work, the resultant behaviour may be distorted and the observers might not get a true picture of what they are trying to observe.

In non-participant situations, observers watch the action, but are separate from it; they could also be in a distanced capacity - from a point of concealment (such as a car), or viewing the action on film. This in itself poses difficulties. If observers operate from a place of hiding, it is very difficult for them to place a value on what they are observing in this abstracted mode: when does a glance become a stare, for instance, or a game turned into a battle of wills? If they are physically within the action context, perhaps operating a video camera in a classroom, they must still acknowledge that their presence will have some effect on the group and possibly distort its behaviour.

Structuring the observation

Real life situations are notoriously difficult to observe and record. The most popular way of recording interaction is by adopting some kind of grid (see for example the Flanders Interaction Analysis Repertoire - Chapters 7 and 11).

In this technique, the action to be observed is broken down into time intervals - two minute blocks, for example. A grid is drawn up according to those blocks, and interactions are noted and tallied within those time blocks. If we are watching the number of times A makes eye contact with B, for instance, we could draw up the following record sheet (note that this example has tally marks to show you what the record sheet might look like):

Record sheet to show amount of eye contact established

Minutes	1	2	3	4	5
eye contact established	ЖЖ ЖЖ ||| II		ЖЖ ЖЖ ЖЖ I	ЖЖ II	ЖЖ ЖЖ

If we wanted to observe the television viewing habits of the family during the evening we might draw up something like this (this example is left blank for you to fill in):

Record sheet to show television viewing habits during an evening

Monday / Kind of programme	Times in half hours					
	7.00-7.29	7.30-7.59	8.00-8.29	8.30-8.59	9.00-9.29	9.30-9.59
comedy						
crime						
news						
sport						
drama						
game show						
other						

We could keep a daily record and build it into a weekly or monthly record.

More examples will be offered in Part Three. The best record sheet to show events or interactions is the one you develop yourself. Although there are a number of charting procedures available, no one is applicable for every study, and you may well have to be adaptive and creative.

Inter-observer (inter-rater/inter-scorer) reliability

In order to make a credible evaluation of the situation, all the observers' perceptions of what is happening must tally. In order to get to this stage, observers need to have practised before the observation task, decided on the criteria they are going to focus on, and agreed procedures for agreeing their perceptions.

They need to ensure reliability by using an appropriate rating scale, and making sure that all the items are valid. For example, they would make not ask for judgements such as 'number of times boy played with toys', when the boy might just have been looking at the toys.

Procedure for conducting an observational study

HOW TO DO . . .

Here is a general action plan for conducting an observational study.

1. Decide on what you want to find out. You need to focus on observing a particular situation, identifying the categories of behaviour that you are interested in (the things people say and do), and counting how many times these specific behaviours occur within the time of your observation.

2. Formulate a hypothesis about the behaviour of the people in the situation you want to observe.

3. Select your sample. Decide on the categories of behaviour that you are interested in observing.

   (If you intend to use this observational study as the basis of a future investigation, think now about variables. Are you suggesting that there might be a causal relationship between the different variables in the situation you are observing? Are there any extraneous variables that you need to take into consideration?)

4. Decide on the type of data gathering technique to use. Draw up a record sheet to gather the raw data. Make sure you provide spaces for different categories of behaviour.

5. Pilot the study. Go to a location similar to the location where you will conduct the study proper. Use your record sheet to test its effectiveness. Keep your rough work.

6. Re-think any weaknesses in overall design. Refine the record sheet, changing any unsatisfactory items, or eliminating them and adding new ones.

7. Decide on a time and place for conducting your observation.

8. Conduct the observation.

9. Consider and organise your results on your record sheets. Draw up a table to show the results, particularly showing the different categories of behaviour.

10. Consider your findings. Will you keep your initial hypothesis, or reject it? Does previous literature have any bearing on it? Can your study make a contribution to the literature? Were there any weaknesses in your overall design, your recording instrument or other documentation, that produced a peculiar result?

11. Write up your report.

Surveys

Surveys are used to gather general opinion from a sample of the population. They are usually quick and easy to administer, and involve the use of questionnaires, interviews, and attitude scales. Advice will be given in chapter 11 on the construction of these.

Surveys have the obvious advantage that they can gather a lot of information fairly quickly. They have in-built disadvantages regarding the complexity of finding the right questions, and also of sample bias.

To avoid sample bias you need to develop a clear action plan for the survey, and ask the same kinds of questions as you are asking throughout this book:

1 What do I want to study?
2 How do I want to study it?
3 Who do I want to ask?
4 How will I evaluate my data?

Question 3 is very important because it will focus on the kind of sample you are seeking. If you want to study (Question 1) the television viewing habits of college students, it is no use selecting a sample of students who are just about to sit their final examinations. They would not be representative of the population.

Surveys lend themselves to sociological enquiry as well as to psychological enquiry, and they can be very useful in gathering opinion to act as a starting point for further investigation. For example, if we were interested in finding out how students react to different teaching methods, we could gather opinion through a survey. Later, perhaps, we could use another technique, such as experimentation or individual case study, to refine our ideas further, depending on what we felt would be the most appropriate methodology.

Procedure for conducting a survey

HOW TO DO . . .

Here is a general action plan for conducting a survey.

1. Decide on what you want to find out. You need to focus on gathering information about what people feel about a particular issue, and counting their responses to make some generalised comment on public opinion about that issue.

2. Formulate a hypothesis about the particular issue you have identified.

3. Select your sample. Use any of the sampling methods discussed in chapter 5. Consider the suitability of participants and also their availability.

4. Decide on the type of data gathering technique to use. Will you use a questionnaire or attitude scale? Which type (see chapter 8)? Draw up a questionnaire or attitude scale.

5. Decide on the distribution method. Will you issue your document as a self-completion exercise, conduct an interview, or something else? What is your time-scale for the return of documentation?

6. Standardise instructions. Decide on the wording to be given to the participants, both verbally and in the written form. Write this verbatim at the top of the document - that is, write down the actual words spoken, using inverted commas where necessary. Also decide on the wording to thank them, and write this at the bottom of the document. De-brief as thoroughly as possible - thank your participants and explain what the questionnaire is trying to find out.

7. Pilot this rough draft. Try it out on a few friends. Change any items that are not absolutely clear, or replace or eliminate them. Keep the pilot work.

8. Issue the questionnaire, according to what you decided above.

9. If you decide to interview people, arrange a time and place with them. Conduct the interview at the designated time and place.

10. Use an appropriate record sheet to record their responses. This may well be a blank questionnaire, although you may also devise an accompanying record sheet as well.

11. Consider and organise the results on your record sheets. Draw up a table to show the results.

12. Consider your findings. Will you keep your hypothesis or reject it? Can you relate your study to the literature? Can your study make a contribution to the literature? Were there any weaknesses in your overall design that produced a peculiar result?

13. Write the report.

Case study

Case study uses qualitative rather than quantitative research methods.

Until quite recently case study was regarded as somewhat unscientific. It focuses on individual cases, and documents progress through life, usually in terms of one or two specific criteria. It was held to be unscientific because individual case studies had little reliability so could not be used to draw general conclusions about human behaviour. Recently opinion has started to move away from the purpose of psychological enquiry being only on trying to explain - or explain away - human behaviour, and is now trying to understand individual behaviour by looking at the kinds of intentions people have when they act in the way that they do.

Case study is valuable here. It can look at one or two individuals and keep detailed records of their progress within a specific area of their life - say improvement in memory, or in learning readiness. As a researcher you may take a participant or non-participant stand. If participant, you must acknowledge, as in observational studies, that you are part of the action and will influence the action and results simply by being present. If you are a participant, you will need to develop techniques such as using diaries and logs to record progress, as well as interviews to see how progress is going (see chapter 10). If you are non-participant you will depend on the people in the study keeping careful records of personal progress which you will collate and interpret, either alone or in collaboration with the others in the study.

Although case study is not yet part of all GCSE work, we are discussing it here as it is gaining in popularity, and could well add to the work you are doing in your GCSE studies.

Procedure for conducting a case study

HOW TO DO . . .

1. Decide on the area you wish to investigate. Try to identify one or two aspects of the area that you are particularly interested in studying.

2. Select the person or persons you wish to study.

3. Decide on whether you are to be participant or non-participant in the study.

4. Decide on the kind of data gathering techniques to be used: diaries, audio/videotape recordings. This is your raw data. Keep these records yourself, and ask your participants to do so as well.

5. Arrange to visit or otherwise interact with the person(s) you are studying at intervals. Keep a record of these interactions.

6. Keep a 'critical incidents' log. Pull out of the raw data any critical incidents that are symptomatic of the aspects you identified at (1). Show any change in the nature of that aspect that indicates development.

7. Evaluate your findings. Can you show a 'before and after' scenario? Can you present clear evidence of the 'before' and 'after' events to show a progression or development?

8. Evaluate your methodology. Have you conducted a rigorous analysis of the situation you have been involved in? Is the study merely anecdotal, or have you rooted the anecdote in a wider consideration of the aspect you have been studying? Were there any weaknesses in your own procedure and analysis that could be improved?

9. Write the report.

7 RECORD SHEETS

The methodological emphasis in your coursework is on quantification - that is, giving a number value to events and phenomena and then analysing these numerical values. When you produce documentary evidence, therefore, you need to assign a numerical value to every phenomenon that you are studying, and then develop careful record sheets to show how those values may be noted for further analysis - for example, in a conversation, how many times did a person smile, or say 'yes', or initiate the conversation.

Record sheets come in a variety of guises. We'll present some of the most common here. You are encouraged, however, to develop your own for your specific purposes, and to be as creative as possible to capture the kind of evidence you feel is appropriate within the type of study you are conducting. The kinds of record sheets we shall discuss here use the methods of audio-visual recording, head-counting, interaction-process analysis, procedural analysis, and interaction charting (such as sociometry).

Audiovisual records

Audio and videotape recordings are an efficient way of gathering evidence, but very time consuming and expensive. This kind of recording acts as a primary data source - you actually capture the action on tape, rather than translate it into other symbols, such as tally marks on a record sheet. Its interpretation can be problematic, and also its presentation to a wider audience. In your GCSE project, you would have to translate it for the reader into quantitative terms. On the whole, this kind of recording is too sophisticated for what we need at GCSE, though it can be invaluable at higher levels of study.

Head counting

We do a head count simply when we wish to record the number of times a certain event or phenomenon occurred. Say, for instance, you wanted to study postural echoing, the phenomenon where a person adopts the same bodily posture as another person who s/he is talking to. You could go, say, to a restaurant, an airport waiting lounge, or other public place where people interact, and record the number of people who were demonstrating postural echoing (this record sheet has been filled in):

Record sheet to record number of incidences of postural echoing

	Saturday 13.9.93 8.00-8.30 The Fisher Pub Lounge	Tuesday 18.10.93 7.30-8.00 Heathrow Departure Lounge	Friday 10.11.93 7.30-8.00 Carly's Coffee Shop
body stance e.g. arms folded	JHT JHT II	JHT JHT JHT JHT JHT II	JHT JHT II
non-verbal cues e.g. headnodding	JHT JHT JHT JHT II	JHT JHT JHT II	JHT JHT JHT JHT II

This kind of tally sheet simply records the number of times a unit of behaviour is demonstrated within a certain time, the unit of behaviour here being arms folded and headnodding.

Notice this easy way of counting, called a five-bar gate. You simply make four strokes and then cross them through to make up a unit of five.

Interaction-process analysis

There are a number of systems available to show us how to conduct interactional analysis. The idea is to capture the interactions between people, and to quantify the interactions. The most common ways to capture those interactions is, following Flanders, to define categories of behaviour and record the number of times the behaviours are demonstrated within time blocks. This is what you need to do to fulfil skills A12 and B10. So, say you were trying to analyse the interactions in a conversation between two people as part of your observational study, you could propose several categories of behaviour, and then record them, at 1-minute intervals. Your categories could be:

Record sheet to analyse conversation interactions

	1-minute intervals				
	1	2	3	4	5
categories of behaviour					
smiles					
touches					
nods					
initiates conversation					
listens					
and so on ...					

This exercise is very demanding in concentration. You need to be familiar with the categories you have devised. The more categories of behaviour you are looking at, the more difficult it is to record them. The exercise is intensive and cannot be sustained for long.

Try devising a record sheet that would go with an observational study, an experiment and a survey. Devise your own categories of behaviour and time allocations. A GCSE project need not be elaborate. You should look for four, five or six categories of behaviour, and record their occurrence.

Procedural analysis

This kind of exercise requires you to draw up an agenda, or time plan of a specific event, and then to plot the actions and interactions within the frame. For example, imagine you wish to see who speaks most at a Governors' meeting. You would draw up a table like this:

Governor	Number of contributions
Mr Davis	
Mrs Green	
Mr Farthing	
Mr Golightly	
Mrs McDonald	
Ms Nicholas	
Miss Oppenheimer	
Mr Wallasy	

Time sampling

If you have not a great deal of time available, you might decide to use a time sampling procedure - that is, short intervals of time interspersed throughout longer periods of time. For example, if you were observing driver behaviour, you might observe from 9.00-9.30 a.m. over a period of days, or choose the same time during one or two days over a period of weeks. Or you might observe from 9.00-9.15 a.m., 2.00-2.15 p.m. and 6.00-6.15 p.m. within the one day.

Time sampling is particularly appropriate to observational studies.

Interaction charting

This is probably too sophisticated for GCSE, but it is offered here out of general interest and use value.

There are a number of ways to capture actions and interactions in chart form. The literature of group developmental work is rich in these kinds of ideas. This is where observers chart the relationships among people in groups:

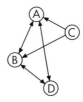

Clearly B is very popular, while C seems to be isolated. This kind of exercise can be useful in getting various people's reactions to group relationships.

It is also possible to observe and organise the 'traffic' of group relationships with schemes based on the same principle:

Class 1

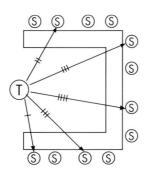

Class 2

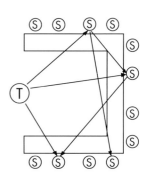

In the classroom diagrams, T is the teacher and S is the student. In class 1 there is a teacher-centred situation. The teacher controls the traffic and it is all one-way. There is no interaction between students. The lines across the arrows indicate the number of times T and Ss interact. In class 2 the teacher still controls the traffic, but now sets up interactions between Ss. In class 3, the teacher has delegated authority to S6 who now sets up interactions with other students. In class 4 the teacher has re-arranged the social relationships, has changed the geography of the classroom, and has changed role to become a participant.

Class 3

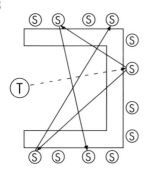

Class 4

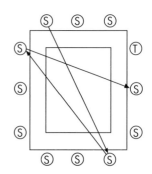

This kind of interpersonal charting is very useful in professional development programmes where people have to observe their own movements to increase their awareness of what they are doing and how they might improve their performance.

This is a very small selection of possible record sheets. (It would be a good idea, when everyone in the class has reached the stage of data gathering, for them to produce a pilot plan of a record sheet and to share it with the class to get feedback and possible new ideas. Brainstorming can be useful here.)

Do not be afraid of inventing new ways to record the data you are gathering. Only you can create a document that will be entirely appropriate to your own individual study.

This aspect of drawing up record sheets will be continued in chapter 11, when we shall also consider the kind of tables that might be appropriate for presenting an analysis of findings.

⑧ QUESTIONNAIRES AND ATTITUDE SCALES

There are a number of good books available on constructing questionnaires and attitude scales. In this chapter we want to offer some basic guiding principles, all of which are rooted in common sense, along with some ideas of what not to do.

Planning

Always plan first rather than make it up as you go along. Remember that, in answering questionnaires, people operate out of good will. They don't have to give up their time and energy, so please respect this by asking questions which actually can be answered, and by avoiding questions which are irritating or redundant, such as 'Which sex are you?' - particularly if gender makes no difference in your study - or 'Are you young, middle-aged or old?' (Yes, it really has appeared on a questionnaire!)

Your planning can take the form of a series of decisions, as in the flow diagram:

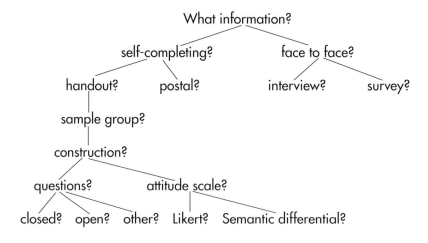

Decision 1: What information do you need?

Decide what the minimum information is that you need and do not ask any more. If any aspect is unnecessary, such as age, gender, race, do not ask a question about it. Answering questions takes time. If people have to answer too many questions, they will not answer, or will get fed up and give inaccurate answers, or not return the questionnaire, and so on. The information you are looking for is relevant and meaningful to your project. You are not interested in any other information.

Decision 2: Self-completing or for use in interviews?

Is the questionnaire self-completing or is it designed for a face-to-face situation? If it is for face-to-face encounters, the same principles of questionnaire construction as outlined in this chapter will apply, but you will also have to bear in mind the skills of interviewing. That aspect is dealt with in chapter 9, 'Interviews'.

Decision 3: Is the self-completing questionnaire used as a handout or is it posted?

Postal surveys are very costly. They are used usually in medium to large scale research projects, and so you probably don't need to go down that road.

For GCSE you will probably aim to construct a questionnaire that may be used with a sample of 10-20 persons. You are probably aiming to produce a self-completing questionnaire that may be handed out to family, friends and colleagues.

Decision 4: Who is going to answer it?

You need to give thought here as to who your sample group will be. Remember that the sample group is notionally representative of the whole population, and will demonstrate the characteristics that you are studying. Remember also that you can choose your sample group through a variety of techniques (random, quota or opportunity sampling techniques and so on: skill A8). You also need to consider the availability of resources (skill A9). Who is available? Where will you find them? How will you approach them? How will you assure them of confidentiality and their right to withdraw or not to answer (skill B8)?

Decision 5: How will you construct the questionnaire?

Do you want to set the agenda and get back specific answers to specific questions? Do you want the respondents to be free to answer as they wish? How much control will you build in? These questions depend on the kind of information you are looking for. If you want back fairly stereotyped information and focused answers, you will opt for a restricted answering format, such as ticking a particular box which contains a pre-specified answer. If you want a more general opinion-based response, you will ask a question such as, 'What do you think about ... ?', but then you have the task of interpreting the information and classifying it and coding it into categories for your data analysis and presentation. (Note that this would not qualify for marks for skills A12 and B10.) Ticking boxes is much easier, for researcher and respondent, though less imaginative.

Decision 6: Do you want to use a question-type format or an attitude scale?

Will you ask questions that are seeking opinion or information, or will you ask questions that are gauging attitude? There is much overlap here, but a general rule is this: if you want feedback on opinion and/or information, you should construct items that require some kind of knowledge-based response, whereas if you want feedback regarding people's attitudes, you could operate a scale system to judge the degree of feeling involved.

Collingwood (1939) says that there are no 'true' answers. There are only 'right' or 'appropriate' answers that will keep the dialogue open. The same idea applies to questions. There are no 'correct' questions, but there are 'right' or 'appropriate' questions that will keep the conversation going by giving us answers that are relevant and meaningful. It is necessary, then, always to focus on the criteria, '*Is this question appropriate? Is it going to give me the kind of feedback that will help me to move my thinking forward?*'

Decisions in constructing questionnaires

Now you have a series of decisions to make in deciding on appropriate questions. Some of the most common decisions are listed here. You will probably discover more for yourselves.

1   Question type - closed or open?

Closed and fixed response type questions

The easiest type of question to answer is a closed question, such as

	Yes	No
Do you smoke?	☐	☐

Another easy kind of question to answer is a fixed-response type question, such as

(i) My current marital status is   (a) unmarried   ( )
                                   (b) married   ( )
                                   (c) widowed   ( )
                                   (d) separated   ( )
                                   (e) divorced   ( )
                                   (f) other (please state)

(tick one only)

(ii) My age is: (a) under 15; (b) 15-19; (c) 20-24; (d) 25-29; (e) 30-34; (f) 35-39 (circle one only).

Danger points:

Beware of putting your own assumptions into questions:

For example: How many children have you?   (1);   (2);   (3)?
(*The respondent might not have any.*)

Beware of ambiguously worded items:

For example: Which age group are you? (a) under 15; (b) 15-19;
(c) 20-25; (d) 25-30; (e) 30-35?
(Respondents who are 15, 25 and 30 would not know which category to opt for.)

Open ended questions

These types of questions offer the respondent the opportunity to discuss options more: for example,

1 Do you use any of the following washing powders?
(a) Brand A; (b) Brand B; (c) Brand C?

2 If you do, please say why you used that one.
....
....

As well as offering the respondent a wider option, open-ended questions give you a greater interpretation task. In interpreting the answers, you would have to allocate answers into categories and enumerate them. But beware - allocating answers into categories will NOT earn skills A12 or B10 - these come only through observing behaviour.

This point is discussed further in Part Four. Open-ended questions may potentially offer richer feedback, but they make life more difficult for you as researcher. Remember also - if you ask open ended questions, put dotted lines in for the answer to limit its length. Some respondents will be only too happy for the chance to write on!

Danger points:

Most of the points dealt with for fixed-choice questions apply here as well. However, there are certain danger points particularly associated with open-ended questions. These include:

Leading questions

Do you not agree that as a society we ought to make people conform to our expectations?

(Well, no, I don't actually, because I believe in individuals' rights to liberty and freedom of thinking. However, if you put it that way, I suppose you want me to answer 'yes'.)

Hypothetical questions

If you were rich, would you give up work?

(*Does work have to do with wealth, or earning a living? Can't work be enjoyable just for its own sake? Don't we need to live productive lives? Is work to be seen only as labour? Besides, what do you mean by rich? What do you mean by work?*)

Sexist questions

What would you do if you were given the job and then became pregnant?

(*Would you put that question to a man?*)

This last point raises a whole number of issues to do with stereotyping and prejudice. Questionnaires often communicate cultural norms, such as:

	White	Black	Asian	Other	(please specify)
What nationality are you?					

(*Are the first three seen as most important? Why does white come first?*)

Beware of ambiguity (more than one meaning) or careless wording in your items: for example -

Where do you study?

school	☐
college	☐
evening institute	☐
university	☐

(*I might study at college in the day and evening institute in the evening. I might be taking a distance learning course while working.*)

How would you describe your feelings towards joy-riders?

They should be punished	( )
They should be imprisoned	( )
They should be cautioned	( )
They should be made to do community service	( )

(Tick one only)

(*There could be all kinds of interpretations here. Some respondents might want to have a 'sliding scale' of punishments, but the choice of wording constrains them.*)

Beware double questions: for example:

Which football team do you support? (a) Manchester United; (b) Sheffield; (c) Arsenal?

(*Excuse me, I have never been interested in football.*)

Beware double negatives: for example:

In your opinion, do mothers who do not work not qualify for some kind of income from the state?

(*Pardon?*)

There are many other difficulties lying in wait for questionnaire setters. Good advice is to construct your own questionnaire and then pilot it on a few friends and family. Replace or take out any items that are suspect. Pilot it again until you are reasonably sure that the questionnaire works as you might want it to. Don't forget to place your rough work in your appendices in order to earn skill mark B6.

Decisions in constructing attitude scales

If you are seeking feedback regarding attitudes, it is often easier to construct attitude scales rather than use question-based questionnaires. Attitude scales usually make statements and ask the respondent to indicate where her or his answer will be along a specific scale. Although the items are presented as statements, attitude scales fall into the 'questionnaire' category, and will therefore earn the mark at skill A5.

There are a number of different types of scales, but the two most popular are these:

Likert-type scale

	Strongly agree	Agree	Don't know	Disagree	Strongly disagree
Women are more careful drivers than men					

There is divided opinion about whether to include the middle rank. Some people feel that this category does not achieve very much in terms of feedback and can best be left out. You should decide what is most appropriate for your purposes.

Semantic differential

This is often used to test people's emotional responses to certain concepts. Aspects of the concept or attitude-object are polarised against each other along a scale, and the respondent is asked to mark where s/he feels an answer is appropriate: for example:

Teachers are

good	__	✔	__	__	__	__ bad
caring	__	✔	__	__	__	__ harsh
responsible	✔	__	__	__	__	__ irresponsible

These two types of scale may also be mixed, as on many self-perception or social awareness exercises: for example:

	A lot like me	Something like me	Not sure	Not like me	Not at all like me
I am a good listener					
I am cheerful					
I am generous					
etc.					

This kind of arrangement is very rigid, and does not allow very much for variation. Recognising that we all have good and bad days, a more flexible kind of answering system for the items could be:

	Always	Sometimes	Usually	Seldom	Never
I am a good listener					
I am cheerful					
I am generous					
etc.					

This kind of scaling is fraught with the danger of misinterpretation, however. I might respond: I am a good listener - always - except when the conversation turns to doing the dishes, and then I switch off.

Your intuition and good common sense must always prevail.

Steps in constructing and administering the questionnaire

DO . . .

> 1   Decide what information you need to find out. Construct your questionnaire. Put the instructions for completing the questionnaire at the top of the paper. Be polite, and ask your participants to help. Say please. Do not assume that they have to give you their time and labour.

2   Clearly handwrite or type your questionnaire. Leave enough space for the respondent to fill it in easily. Clearly number or otherwise annotate your items. Use good quality paper. Do not use scruffy paper, as people may not feel like spending their valuable time and effort on an exercise which clearly has not demanded too much of your valuable time and effort. Pay attention to detail in content and appearance.

3   If you photocopy the questionnaire, make sure that the copies are clear and legible.

4   Pilot the questionnaire (skill B6). Try it out on a few people, and invite their criticism. Listen to the criticism and act on it. Delete or modify any suspect items. Keep your original drafts for submission with your project work to show that you have piloted it. Pilot it again with a different group of 3/4 people. Act on their criticism. Keep any documentation regarding feedback as evidence that you have piloted your questionnaire.

5   Run the questionnaire. Give your respondents a fixed time in which to return the questionnaire. This can vary - 10 minutes or a day or a week. Often people need a little time to become familiar with the items, so do not rush them. Write on the questionnaire itself when you would like it returned. If you want people to send it back to you, provide postage and envelopes.

Important points to remember

Indicate on the questionnaire that answers will remain confidential. Do not ask for names or personal details such as age, unless you need that information. Always let people know that they do not have to answer items if they do not wish to, and that they are always free to opt out. These aspects are important for skill B8, to show that you have your participants' best interests at heart.

At the end of the questionnaire, thank your participants. Make a statement to say that you will inform them of the results, if they so wish, and the part their contribution played in your investigation. This is all part of the de-briefing exercise (B3).

Remember - the courtesies involved in asking people to take part in your work are probably more important than technical accuracy. These are ethical points, and the rule is, 'Do as you would be done by'.

Reference:

Collingwood, R.G., *An Autobiography*, (Oxford University Press, 1939).

⑨ INTERVIEWS

> **NOTE:** Chapters 9 and 10, dealing with interviews and keeping diaries, are not focused on GCSE level work. There are no skill marks awarded for these aspects by the NEAB. However, they are appropriate to psychological research at most levels, and we feel you ought to know about them for future reference. You may skip them if you wish and go straight on to Chapter 11.

Interviews are used in conducting surveys and usually operate in a face-to-face context. Telephone interviews require a whole set of special skills which we shall not go into here. Postal interviews would take the form of questionnaires with pre-set items.

Interviews have distinct advantages over a questionnaire-only method, but they also have inherent disadvantages. The advantages are to do with the fact that you could receive richer feedback as you would be able to ask probing questions to elicit explanations; the disadvantages are mainly to do with researcher effect on the respondent, and also with researcher bias in terms of reliability of responses. More on these issues later.

Types of interview

Interviews may range from fully structured to free discourse.

Fully structured — semi-structured — guided informal — free discourse

Fully structured

This kind of interview is really the face-to-face delivery of a questionnaire. The respondent is not given any flexibility in answering questions or qualifying them in any way. The usual form of the questions is closed:

(a) yes/no type questions: for example, 'Are you married?'
(b) responding to a statement in terms of an attitude scale: for example,

	Strongly agree	Agree	Don't know	Disagree	Strongly disagree
Psychological enquiry is all about understanding human behaviour					

The questions are asked in the same order, and the format never differs.

This is the easiest kind of interview to administer and to score, since it operates on a simple tick-system. Inter-scorer reliability can be high.

Semi-structured

In this kind of interview, the questions are standardised and are asked in a fairly directive way, but the respondent is free to answer with qualification. For example,

'What is your opinion about empirical forms of psychological research?'
'What do you think about criminal mothers being put in prison?'

This kind of open-ended question allows the respondent to answer, 'Yes, but ... ', and also allows the researcher to ask further probing questions, to gain richer insight and data.

Interpreting the data in this kind of interview is very much more subjective, so scorers would need training prior to conducting the interview to agree types of further probing question asked, criteria to be applied in giving a value to answers, and scoring procedure.

Guided informal

This is a much freer interaction which can verge on free dialogue. The interviewer usually has a set of questions to ask at some time during the interview, but the respondent is free to answer as s/he wishes. The interviewer has to keep task-oriented and cover the agenda, but is also free to participate in an informal and unstructured way.

In scoring this kind of interview, it is very difficult to aim for inter-scorer reliability. The way that scorers would evaluate the interviews would be to share their perceptions of what had occurred in terms of the pre-set agenda, and to give an evaluation of each of those questions which could then accumulate to some kind of aggregate score or judgement.

Free discourse

This kind of interview has a starting point but no set agenda. Both interviewer and interviewee would feel entitled to talk about what they wished.

Scoring in this kind of interview is inappropriate. Evaluation methods would be a more subjective interpretation of the events, and people would agree perceptions and understandings rather than scores. What in empirical research would then be checked through inter-scorer reliability would now be agreed through intersubjective agreement, by making joint accounts of interpretations of events available to a wider public.

Conducting the interview

(a)   Data gathering

Ways to collect information from interviews use note-taking, audiotape recording and videotape recording.

Note taking: You need to be efficient at taking notes. This can be helped by developing a personal shorthand or speedwriting. Notebooks can be cumbersome, but you will probably have an agenda or list of questions in any case, and can write notes against the questions.

Audiotape recording: Using audiotape can be particularly useful in surveys or case studies. In order to use audiotape recording, a transcript will have to be made of the conversation. The whole transcript, or excerpts from it, will act as evidence in justifying and reinforcing any points that you are trying to make. Be careful about transcribing. It is a very lengthy procedure, and should be undertaken only if you are sure that this really is the best method to gather the data. The results of including excerpts as evidence can be powerful and have high validity value.

Videotape recording: This is as near to reality as it is currently possible to get. Video will capture all the non-verbal, as well as verbal, messages that are being sent and received by all parties.

The use of video will be ostensive representation in support of what you are saying. If you are aiming to show a change of attitude or behaviour by a certain intervention - say you think a different teaching method might improve the quality of the learning of children - you may show how the children were learning before the new technique was introduced, and then the same children learning after the new technique was introduced - a before and after representation.

(b)   Establishing relationships

1   Be non-judgemental.

As an interviewer you are there to interview, not to judge. Accept what your interviewee has to say, even though you might not agree with it. Your interviewees have given their time to you, so you must honour this, and not expect them to behave as you wish as well. Being accepting means accepting their language, their point of view, their wish to close the interview when they want, not making judgemental responses, not imposing your own values on them. You have asked them to talk; now you must honour the fact that they are talking and respect what they have to say. It is your job to make them feel at ease, not the other way round.

2   Ethical considerations

You must always ensure that you follow good ethical practice. Tell your interviewee what the interview is about. If you do not want them to know what it is about, you must tell them this as well, but reassure them that you will let them know later (skill B8). It is unethical to mislead or deceive people without later telling them the truth, or without letting them know at the beginning that they have the right to withdraw or not to answer any questions they are not entirely comfortable with. You must also assure them of complete confidentiality, and you must honour this confidentiality. You must never divulge to anyone what you are told. It will always come out somewhere if you do!

3   Your own self-conduct

You should try to appear supportive but fairly neutral. It is almost impossible to be entirely neutral, and it questionable in any case if interviewees expect the interviewer to be neutral. We tend to be more comfortable with a person who is honest, acknowledges that s/he does not necessarily agree with us, but is committed to respecting what we have to say than with someone who puts on a show of neutrality. For someone not to be transparent with us, while we are being transparent with them, puts us on the defensive. Aim to offer a view of yourself as a caring, supportive listener, operating in a non-judgemental capacity rather than in a value-free capacity. Throughout the interview you must try to communicate that you value what the interviewee has to say.

4   Language

This means adopting the form of language that is appropriate to the situation. Do not try to talk down - or up - to the interviewee. Try to adopt the same level. This does not mean picking up the same slang expressions or jargon particular to that culture, but by the same token it does mean not expecting the interviewee to pick up the jargon particular to your culture. Your interviewee will not expect you to use, for example, their brand of street language, or computer language, or playground language; equally, you should not expect them to use research language or techniques of data gathering language. It is all a question of using common sense to decide what is appropriate in this situation to keep the discussion going. This brings us to specific interviewing skills.

(c)   Interviewing skills

Interviewing skills are grounded in your personal and interpersonal skills. These are not so much the technical skills of constructing and administering the research process as counselling skills. You are the key person here.

Interviewing involves real one-to-one relationships. Your performance will decide whether it is a successful interview or not. Here are some of the most common interviewing skills. Try videotape recording yourself, and practise these skills in role play or actual interview situations.

Listening skills

The art of good interviewing is in being prepared to get the other person to talk. The main aim of interviews is for you to find out what the other person thinks, not to air your own opinions.

Active listening means being aware of body language, including stance, maintaining eye-contact, non-verbal gestures which all communicate the message, 'I value what you have to say. I am really interested in you.' This means also not fiddling with papers and pens, not picking your nails, but sitting or standing still quietly while focusing your attention on your interviewee, to indicate that you want to hear what s/he has to say.

Verbal support

Encouraging words and phrases will make your interviewee feel more at ease and therefore more likely to chat, giving you a richer insight into her or his opinion. Don't let the interviewee talk at length without some kind of response from you, even if this is murmurs or 'Mm's'. Try to put yourself in the other person's shoes; how would you feel under these circumstances?

Playback

Sometimes an interview can falter because the interviewee is not sure how to continue. A really helpful technique can be to playback what the speaker has just said. For example, you might say, '*Now, as I understand it, you are saying that you feel that you were a victim of bullying at school.*' It can move the conversation forward quite significantly if you then go on with a gentle probing question: '*Would you like to say how you felt about that?*' What you must never do here, in your eagerness to keep the whole thing going, is to make unwarranted interpretations about what the speaker has just said, or to adopt a stance that the speaker might find threatening: '*Does that mean that you have been socially damaged, then?*'

Offer insight, not judgement

In order to get people to speak about themselves, you need to offer insight into their feelings, to empathise with what they say. Get them to explore their ideas; do not impose your own. Offer playback like this: '*Can I check with you that I understand what you are saying there? You are saying that … Is that right?*' Do not say things like this: '*Well, as far as I'm concerned, you seem to be saying … and that is clearly illogical.*' End of interview.

Don't be afraid of silences

Silence can be quite threatening, especially to interviewers. It is important to recognise, however, that silences are sometimes important for speakers to gather their thoughts or harness their courage. Do not feel that you have to jump in at the first pause. Aim to develop sensitivity in judging whether a silence means that the speaker is looking for a cue from you to help him or her to re-focus and take the conversation forward, or are they feeling their way intuitively, and need you to remain still and silent - a supportive ally who understands the need to listen and to provide time and space to think.

(d)   Types of question most common

Here are some of the kinds of question you might practise. These are all 'framing questions', that is, not to do with the subject matter (you will already have a schedule for this), but to do with getting the conversation going and sustaining it so that it is a valuable experience for both interviewer and interviewee.

Clarifying questions

- to clarify something that the speaker has said: *'Can I check that, please? I understand you to be saying that ... '*
- to clarify a point about the subject matter: *'You will see that this question is asking for your opinion specifically about ... '*
- to clarify a point of procedure: *'Shall we leave that point till we get to question 6? It's dealt with more fully there.'*
- to clarify when it is appropriate to change the topic or focus: *'I'd like to move on now. Are you comfortable with what we've discussed so far?'*

Probing questions

- to explore an issue that the speaker has raised: *'Can we discuss that a little further?'* or *'Can you just unpack that a little, please?'* or *'Can we explore what you mean by ... ?'*
- to help the speaker move her own thinking forward: *'Does that relate to what you were saying earlier about ... ?'*

Remember not to try to score points: *'But that contradicts what you said before!'* This is not a power relationship; this is a counselling relationship. Your job is to support people in exploring their own thinking, not to trick or trap them.

Context-specific questions:

- to check that the interviewee is at ease with the question: *'Is it all right for us to talk about this?'*
- to check that the interviewee is at ease with the situation: *'Are you comfortable sitting there?'*
- to check that the interviewee understands the question: *'Can I ask you to put that question in your own words?'*
- to check that the interviewee is comfortable with your own performance: *'Have I said that correctly?'*

Remember never to put your speaker in the wrong or under stress; for example, *'Is that clear, or do you need me to explain it again?'* It is your responsibility to make sure that the interviewee feels supported, and that this is a valuable learning experience for you both.

10 KEEPING DIARIES

The usual purpose of keeping a diary (log or journal) is to keep a record of events. In empirical research you will probably use participants' diaries to document progress within the study: that is, you might ask the research participants to keep records of what they are doing, and you will use those diaries as raw data.

You would tend to be an outsider doing research on insiders. This will be true of experiments and investigations where you as outsider researcher aim to show a causal relationship between independent and dependent variables. It is however most unlikely that you would invite your research participants to keep diaries in experiments and investigations. You would probably invite them to take part in this kind of study as members of a sample group so that you could keep a record of their reactions within different conditions of the task under consideration. You would have the job of keeping a diary or log of what was happening.

In observational studies and surveys it is not unusual for researchers to invite participants to keep diaries. The participants would be aiming to record their reactions to a particular circumstance or event over time. The diaries in this sense would act as logs, and would be submitted to you for analysis. You would use the diaries as raw data in an observational study to trace the development of, say, relationships between a group, or in a survey to measure the possibly changing perceptions of attitudes towards a person or another attitude object. This is known as a 'diary method'. A further refinement of this method would be if you wished to use the diary as initial feedback, and then follow up any aspect in an interview with the diary writer. 'Critical incidents' might particularly indicate a significant change or turning point in the situation that you are researching.

This diary method is widely used, particularly in longitudinal research involving observations, surveys and case study. It highlights the need for strict ethical conduct on the part of the researcher. If you wish to use people's diaries, you must observe certain conventions. These would emphasise the need for courteous handling of the diarists who are giving a good deal of time and effort willingly, and who need to be thanked and acknowledged in the research report. It also stresses the need for confidentiality. If the diarist makes his or her work available to you, there must be a clear understanding whether or not the raw data of the diary is to be made public. Confidentiality must be preserved. If you wish to quote or use the material directly, you must ask permission of the diarist first. People must not be named unless they expressly give permission, but should be referenced by fictitious names or initials, and you must make a note to this effect in the introductory pages of the research report. It is your responsibility to say publicly that any interpretations and conclusions drawn from the data are yours.

Analysis of diaries would initially be qualitative - that is, you would make some kind of personal judgement about the content of the diaries, perhaps looking at the frequency of events, perceptions or other phenomena, and then attempt to turn that qualitative judgement into some kind of quantitative analysis. For example, certain aspects of diarists' behaviour might be analysed in terms of categories of behaviour. If the study is about observing the interactions of siblings, for example, and a parent is keeping a diary for you, the children might be categorised in terms of specific behaviour; for example, 'smiled', 'hesitated', 'initiated conversation'. The diary might show that these events increased in quantity over time, which you could analyse and interpret as an increase in sociability and therefore come to some conclusion about developing patterns of sociability among siblings.

PART 4
RECORDING AND PROCESSING THE DATA

The next two chapters look at statistics. Statistics is about collecting and sorting data, and making sense of it in order to draw conclusions and generalisations.

At GCSE you are required to know and use only a limited amount of descriptive statistics. Domain C asks specifically for certain graphical representations - either a graph, or a bar chart, or a histogram. You do not need to do a pie chart or any other kind of graphic. If you do, you will not lose marks, but you will not gain any more marks, either.

Skill D2 requires you to perform calculations on the data. You may choose any two out of the following five aspects: percentages, mean, median, ratio and range. You must do two of these in order to secure the skills mark. In addition, it might be appropriate also to refer to the mode in some data, though this is not essential.

Chapter 13 discusses how to record the data.

Chapter 14 looks at the analysis and processing of the data.

11 RECORDING THE DATA

Statistics is about collecting and analysing information (data), and then making sense of this in order to draw general conclusions. Descriptive statistics is concerned only to describe the data, present it, and draw basic conclusions about the relationship, if any, between variables. Inferential statistics is about testing whether these conclusions are statistically significant and therefore might have some bearing on the population as a whole. At GCSE we are concerned only with descriptive statistics.

In all the kinds of study you could undertake, you will gather information about what people do or say. You will gather that data in terms of numerical scores, which may then be computed to indicate trends. The data will be recorded on tables and charts. In this chapter we can look at the most common ways of recording data for each of the kinds of study so far discussed. As we have noted in Chapter 7, the best record sheets and tables for presenting the data are the ones that you draw up yourself.

We said before that candidates sometimes mistakenly confuse record sheets, which are used for gathering raw data, and tables and charts, which are used for presenting the data. In Chapter 7 we looked at different kinds of techniques we could adopt for gathering the raw data, and the kinds of record sheets we might formulate. In this chapter, we are looking at the accumulated data as it is presented on tables and charts. Very often, the record sheet itself would act as the document that you would use to present the data, but that is not always the case, as we shall see. What follows here are examples of the kinds of tables and charts that you could develop for presenting your accumulated and processed raw data.

Experiments

Example 1

This experiment is testing the Stroop effect. It uses an unrelated samples design.

Group 1 is shown a series of 20 words all written in the colour that the word is stating: the word 'green' is written in green, for example; 'red' is written in red, and so on. Group 2 is shown a series of 20 words, but each word is written in a colour contrary to what the word is saying. 'Green' is written in black, 'red' is written in blue, and so on. Participants are asked to say what colour they see (not read the word they see) as soon as they perceive it. A stop watch is used to calculate the time between presentation of stimulus and correct spoken response.

Recording the Data

Here is an example of a record sheet.

Time in seconds between presentation of stimulus and correct spoken response

seconds	1	2	3	4	5	6	7	8	9	10	
Group 1 Person											
A	x										
B		x									
C	x										
D				x							
E		x									
F			x								
											TOTAL **13**
Group 2 Person											
G		x									
H			x								
I		x									
J				x							
K			x								
L	x										
											TOTAL **15**

Now here is an example of a table which might go with the record sheet.

Table to show the time in seconds between presentation of stimulus and correct spoken response

	Time taken to respond (in seconds)
Group 1 Participant A B C D E F	1 2 1 4 2 3
TOTAL 13	
Group 2 Participant G H I J K L	2 3 2 4 3 1
TOTAL 15	
	MEAN: Group 1: 13÷6=2.2 Group 2: 15÷6=2.5

Having drawn up this table, you could now compare the scores of the two groups.

Example 2

This experiment is to see whether pictures presented simultaneously with a word help children to recognise the word. The experimenter presents one set of flash cards of words with a picture to one group of children, and another set without the picture to a different group:

Recording the Data

After several learning sessions with the cards, the children in both groups are tested. Only cards without pictures are presented to the children in both groups. How many words can the children 'read'?

Record sheet for each child to show the number of words recognised with pictures

	WORD WITH PICTURE	SCORE
Learning phase	A	
	B	
	C	
	D	
	E	
	F	
	G	
		TOTAL ____

Record sheet for each child to show the number of words recognised without pictures

	WORD WITHOUT PICTURE	SCORE
Learning phase	A	
	B	
	C	
	D	
	E	
	F	
	G	
		TOTAL ____

Record sheet for each child in test phase to show number of words recognised without pictures

	WORD WITHOUT PICTURE	SCORE
Test phase	A	
	B	
	C	
	D	
	E	
	F	
	G	
		TOTAL ____

You could now draw up a table to present your findings:

Table of results to show number of words correctly recognised by each child in each group

	Group 1	Score	Group 2	Score
Child	1		11	
	2		12	
	3		13	
	4		14	
	5		15	
	6		16	
	7		17	
	8		18	
	9		19	
	10		20	
TOTAL				
MEAN				

Example 3

Look at the work presented on page 138. This is an excellent example of a table to present information gathered during an experiment.

Investigations

Example 4

This is an investigation to test whether key word scheme books encourage gender stereotyping. Potential stereotypical categories could be identified as: characteristics, interests, and depicted in situations.

> Girls: *Characteristics:* quiet, helpful, kind, home-loving;
> *Interests:* home-making, dolls, handicrafts;
> *Typical situations:* in the kitchen, shopping with mother.

> Boys: *Characteristics:* naughty, noisy, adventurous, awkward;
> *Interests:* sport, action games, mechanical toys;
> *Depicted in situations:* helping father with the car, working in the garden.

The way in which the information was gathered about perceptions of gender stereotyping was through interviews. The data was then collated, and presented in the table below.

Table to show frequencies of stereotypical characteristics and situations in a book:

	Incidences of stereotypical characteristics	Incidences of stereotypical interests	Incidences of stereotypical situations
Girls			
Boys			
	Incidences of non-stereotypical characteristics	Incidences of non-stereotypical interests	Incidences of non-stereotypical situations
Girls			
Boys			

NOTE: This would not earn skills A12 or B10.

Example 4

An investigation into gender roles in doing the housework. The focus of the investigation is that males will share household duties, but will abstain from doing the more menial tasks such as cleaning the toilet. The information was gathered through the use of questionnaires. The information obtained is presented in the chart below.

Table to show number of household tasks undertaken by males and females

Task	Males	Females
shopping		
feeding the baby		
feeding the children		
washing up		
loading the dishwasher		
dusting		
vacuuming		
cleaning the toilet		
washing the car		
ironing		
decorating		
cooking		
N =		
MEAN =		

Observational studies

Example 5

This is a non-participant observational study to investigate superstitious behaviour. The observer stands at a street corner, near where a ladder has been placed on the pavement leaning against the wall of a building. The observer notes whether people walk round or under the ladder. The observation lasts for one hour.

Record sheet to show the number of people who walked round or under a ladder

	Time in minutes			
	1-15	16-30	31-45	46-60
Observed behaviour walked under ladder				
walked round ladder				

This information may then be translated into a table:

Table to show numbers of people who walked round or under a ladder during one hour

Walked under ladder	Walked round ladder	Total observed
25	52	77

You could compare your results, do calculations on your data, and come to some provisional conclusions about the degree to which superstition appears to influence our lives. This could also be extended to look at gender differences in superstitious behaviour.

Note: this could also earn skill A12 and B10.

Example 6

This observation focuses on the interactions of children at play. It is to investigate the degree of aggression and submission demonstrated within an identified group of 10 children. The times are broken down into 3 minute chunks. Categories of behaviour are identified. The children are observed separately and their behaviour is assigned to the different categories (skills A12 and B10).

Record sheet to show aggressive and submissive behaviours of children at play

CHILD A	Time in blocks of 3 minute intervals				
categories of behaviour	1-3	4-6	7-9	10-12	13-16
shows aggression	III	IIII			
shouts at people	III	IIII	II	I	
pushes and shoves					
is threatening	III	II	IIII	I	II
shows submission					
retreats from others					
is pushed and shoved					
is submissive					

Now translate this information into a table:

Table to show frequencies of aggressive and submissive behaviour by child A

Categories of behaviour	**frequencies**
shows aggression	8
shouts at people	11
pushes and shoves	0
is threatening	13
shows submission	0
retreats from others	0
is pushed and shoved	0
is submissive	0

It seems apparent that Child A is quite aggressive!

Note: In this kind of study you would have to observe children separately. It would be most difficult to attempt to watch more than one person at a time. If you wanted to observe all 10 children you would draw up 10 separate observation schedules, one for each child. In one half hour session of play you could probably observe only five children in detail to obtain any kind of meaningful feedback.

Example 7

To test the hypothesis that adults are more likely to use a pedestrian crossing and not dodge through traffic when they are accompanied by children, this observer stood near a pedestrian crossing for an hour, either during the morning or afternoon, over a period of a week. She collated her data on the following chart:

Record sheet to record number of pedestrians using a crossing

USING CROSSING	
<u>ADULTS WITH CHILDREN</u>	<u>ADULTS ALONE</u>

DODGING TRAFFIC	
<u>ADULTS WITH CHILDREN</u>	<u>ADULTS WITHOUT CHILDREN</u>

This information may be translated into the following table:

Table to show behaviour of adults using a pedestrian crossing during an hour's observation

	Using pedestrian crossing	Dodging traffic
Adults with children	115	24
Adults alone	62	37

Surveys

Example 8

Here is an example of a fixed response questionnaire. It is designed to gather information about people's ice cream eating habits.

Please tick one box only

	Yes	No	Unsure
1 Do you like ice cream?	☐	☐	☐
2 Do you prefer vanilla to chocolate?	☐	☐	☐
3 Do you eat ice cream every day?	☐	☐	☐

The questionnaire could go on to ask 10-20 items.

Let us imagine that the questionnaire is presented to 25 people. The resulting table could offer the following information:

Chart to show preferences for ice cream

Type of ice cream	Preference in percentages
Vanilla	26
Chocolate	13
Strawberry	10
Raspberry ripple	6

and so on ...

Example 9

An example of a fixed response and open ended item questionnaire appears at the end of the chapter. You will see in this example that there are also free response items. Note that the questionnaire constructor limited the amount that the respondent could write by offering only a certain amount of space.

The same effect can be obtained by putting lines alongside or underneath the response: for example,

What do you think about this course? ....
....

EXERCISE

Draw up an appropriate chart or charts to collate and show the data represented on the questionnaire. Do the same for example 10.

Example 10

Here is an open response questionnaire. Note the allocated space for the respondents to write in:

1 Which soap operas do you most frequently watch? (a) ....
(b) ....
(c) ....

2 Why do you watch these more than others? ....

....

3 Which one has the best story line? ....

4 Which has the most true-to-life characters? ....

5 Name any other reason why you might watch the programme you have
chosen. ....

....

Attitude scales

Attitude scales usually make a statement and then invite the respondent to rate his
or her response along a scale. The Likert-type scale is most commonly used.

Example 11

This is an attitude scale to test people's attitudes to leisure time activities.

	Strongly agree 1	Agree 2	Don't know 3	Disagree 4	Strongly disagree 5
1 I like watching television 2 I like going to discos 3 I like ice skating ... and so on ...					

The words may sometimes change to accommodate variations in answers:

	Very often 1	Often 2	Usually 3	Seldom 4	Never 5
1 I am cheerful 2 I am outgoing 3 I am generous ... and so on ...					

The problem with this kind of fixed response item is that there is little room for
flexibility. In the item 'I am cheerful' the answer may be, '*Always, except when I
have run out of cash and have to catch the bus home*', in which case the respondent
has difficulty in giving an honest answer, and your feedback is not absolutely
accurate. This kind of difficulty may be overcome by using a more open-ended
kind of attitude scale such as the example at the top of page 106.

The DORSET EDUCATION PARTNERSHIP

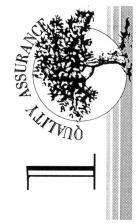

DORSET County Council
Quality Services for local people

Dorset Adult Education Service

Course & Centre
review

QUALITY ASSURANCE

We are committed to building a Service which symbolises quality and value. We should like your help in completing this brief questionnaire now that you have been attending the centre for a few weeks. The form is anonymous and the results of the questionnaire will be evaluated to identify ways in which we could improve the service we offer to all students.

The questionnaire which will take only a couple of minutes to complete, asks about your experiences in getting on to this course.

Name of Course ....

Course Number .... Date ....

DORSET COUNTY COUNCIL

---

9. Is this the first course you have attended in this Adult Education Area ?

☐ Yes   ☐ No

10. Have you attended an Adult Education course in Dorset before ?

☐ Yes   ☐ No

11. Have you attended an Adult Education course in any other county before ?

☐ Yes   ☐ No

12. Which of the following were important in attracting you to this Centre ? *Not all may apply to your course, You can tick more than one box.*

☐ Timing of course

☐ Course leads to National Qualification

☐ Course has a good reputation locally

☐ Course near to where you live

☐ Gives opportunity for employment

☐ Course uses latest technology

☐ Other, please specify [   ]

13. Do you feel you are on the right course

☐ Yes   ☐ No   ☐ Not Sure

14. How far have you travelled to get to this Centre ?

☐ Less than 3 miles   ☐ 3-5 miles   ☐ 5-10 miles   ☐ 10-20 miles   ☐ Over 20 miles

15. How do you travel to this Centre?

☐ Walk   ☐ Cycle/motorcycle   ☐ Car   ☐ Bus   ☐ Other

16. Your Postcode: [   ]
This will help us to identify localities that are not being served

Thank You For Your Help

1. How did you find out about this course ? *Tick only one box*

- [ ] Saw it in the Adult Education Brochure
- [ ] From a person who had attended the course previously
- [ ] From the course tutor
- [ ] Attended the course last year
  If yes, for how many years have you attended this course ? [ ]
- [ ] Newspaper advert
- [ ] Adult Education display/exhibition
- [ ] Adult Education Guidance Service
- [ ] Training Access Points (TAP)
- [ ] Other, please specify [ ]

2. Where did you obtain your copy of the Adult Education Brochure from

- [ ] Library. If so, which library [ ]
- [ ] Collected from the Adult Education Centre
- [ ] By post directly from the Adult Education Centre
- [ ] Post Office. If so which one ? [ ]
- [ ] From a community centre . If so which one ? [ ]
- [ ] From a doctor's or a dentist's surgery.
- [ ] From a Job Centre. If so, which one ? [ ]
- [ ] From a friend
- [ ] Other, please specify [ ]

3. Did you try to get a copy of the brochure from anywhere else ?

Yes [ ] No [ ]

If yes, where did you try ?

---

4. Did you seek any further information (other than that contained in the brochure) to help you decide on this course.

Yes [ ]   No [ ]

If 'Yes' did you do any of the following ?

- [ ] Read the Course Information Sheet
- [ ] Phone the Adult Education Centre for Advice
- [ ] Speak to the tutor
- [ ] Speak to a person who had attended the course previously
- [ ] Contact the Adult Guidance Service
- [ ] Other, please specify [ ]

5. How did you enrol ?

- [ ] In Person by attending the Centre
- [ ] By phone
- [ ] By post
- [ ] A person on my behalf
- [ ] By Fax

6. If you enrolled by phone or in person how helpful did you find the Centre staff ?

- [ ] Very helpful
- [ ] Slightly helpful
- [ ] Not much help
- [ ] Definitely unhelpful

7. How did you find the course enrolment procedure ?

- [ ] Clear & simple
- [ ] Quite clear
- [ ] Reasonably clear
- [ ] Too difficult

8. Have you any suggestions as to how we could improve the enrolment procedure ?

Please Turn Over

We are grateful to Mr Tim Challis and the Dorset Adult Education Service for permission to reproduce this questionnaire here, and acknowledge that it was based on work undertaken by Avon County Council in developing their Further Education Quality Assurance scheme.

Please add any further
comment as necessary

I am cheerful   (a) always, but ....

                            (b) often, but ....

                            (c) usually, but ....

                            (d) seldom, but ....

                            (e) never, but ....

There is also some doubt about whether the middle point, usually denoting 'don't know', is useful, as it does not really provide any kind of valuable feedback. If it does not serve a purpose, leave it out.

Case studies

The main method of gathering information in case studies is through the use of ostensive data, diaries and logs. Which data are significant will depend on the focus of the investigation. For example, if you are studying the developing sociability of a child, you would identify certain criteria whereby you could judge sociability to have been demonstrated - for example, that the child initiated a conversation with another child. You could develop a 'critical incidents' log to take note of these episodes that you felt were significant.

Example 11

Date	Comment
<u>Tuesday, 12th October</u>	
... Susie seems happy enough at school. I am a little worried that she doesn't seem to want to play a great deal	
<u>Wednesday, 13th October</u>	
... Mary is a new girl at school today. Susie seems quite enthusiastic about her, and has asked if she can come home to tea tomorrow ...	Is this a breakthrough?
<u>Thursday, 14th October</u>	
... Susie and Mary get on really well. I was surprised at how supportive Susie can be. I've never seen this side of her before.	A real improvement in sociability!

As noted before, it is unlikely that you will use case study at GCSE, but it is as well to have an insight into what case study involves for your future reference.

12 PROCESSING THE DATA

We saw in Chapter 11 that statistics is about gathering and sorting information (data) and then drawing conclusions from this data. Data may be sorted in two different ways:

1 Variables - the different things, facts or events we are studying;
2 Frequency - the number of things, facts or events we are collecting.

Imagine that someone asked you to sort the contents of your bag, or your locker, or your bathroom cabinet. How would you do this? You would probably empty everything out, sort the items, and make a list of them. This is what happens when shops do a stock-take, for example. They can assess how much they have of any one item, whether they have more of some items than others, and where they need to stock up. You probably do the same with your collection of videos or cassettes before you issue your birthday present list; you check how many you have of any one kind and then ask for something you need.

Here is one way to present this kind of information:

Graph to show contents of handbag

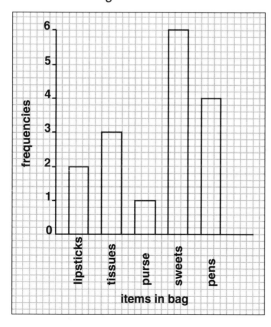

Graph to show different kinds of cassettes

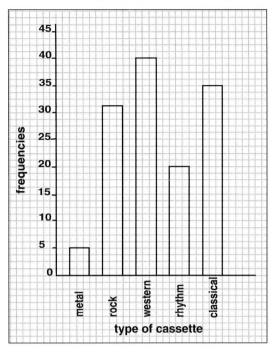

Here is the stock-take information presented in a similar way:

Graph to show number of items in stock

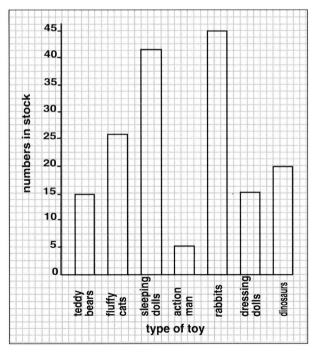

Note: when we draw up graphs like this we usually present the variables along the horizontal axis and the frequencies along the upright axis.

The store manager has a list of the different things he has in stock (the variables) and assesses how many of each item he has (frequency). He uses this information to help him draw a conclusion about his stock level, and let him see whether or not he needs to stock up on any item.

You can come to this kind of overview of what items, or information, you possess, by doing a 'sort and count' exercise such as the following:

Complete the table of how many different kinds of people went into the supermarket between 10.00 a.m. and 10.15 a.m. on Friday, 10th May.

Person	Tally	Frequency
Woman alone		
Woman with one child		
Woman with 2 children		
Woman with more than 2 children		
Man alone		
Man with one child		
Man with 2 children		
Man with more than 2 children		
Child alone		
2 children together		
More than 2 children together		

EXERCISE

Now, construct a graph to show

1   how many different kinds of groups of people went into the supermarket on that particular morning.

Now draw up graphs to show

2   the number of different kinds of shops in the town centre;
3   stock-take of your books, or collection of spoons, thimbles, stamps or other collectables, listing the different kinds you have. The different kinds of things you are looking at are called 'classes' or 'sets'. How many classes have you identified in (1), (2) and (3)?

Discrete and continuous data

In all of these exercises you are counting the data. When we count data we call it **discrete data**. 'Discrete' means separate (nothing at all to do with the word 'discreet' which means 'tactful' or 'prudent'). So we can say that we are counting the pieces of information - these are our discrete data. (A very common mistake here is that candidates draw line graphs to represent discrete data. This is not appropriate: line graphs are used to present continuous data (see below). You would use a bar chart to represent discrete data.)

If we wanted to find out how many people went to the cinema we would count them. If we wanted to find out how many seats there were in the cinema we would count those, too. If, however, we wanted to find out how big the cinema was, we would measure it. When we measure data we call it **continuous data**. Another example of continuous data is the height of your brother, the length of your foot, the time you wake up (you measure time using a clock), temperature changes. All data may be gathered by counting or measuring, and therefore all data are either discrete or continuous. You could look at this another way, and ask the questions 'How much?' (continuous) and 'How many?' (discrete) - for example, 'How much tea?' but 'How many tea bags?'; 'How much time?' but 'How many seconds?'. Discrete variables are self-contained; a discrete scale 1-10 would have each number standing separately - 1, 2, 3, 4, 5, 6, 7, 8, 9, 10. So you could have 1 child, 2 dogs, 3 books, 4 videos, and so on.

Now we could draw up a frequency distribution table, to show how many times the discrete data appeared. So, consider how many shops there are in the town centre:

type of shop	frequency
gift shops	3
bookshops	2
newsagencies	6
clothes shops	9

Continuous data may be presented as a scale that may be divided and sub-divided indefinitely. For example, you could measure your height into metres, then centimetres, then millimetres, then milli-millimetres, and so on indefinitely. Continuous data can have any value in a given range.

The kind of demarcation zones that are used in organising continuous data are called class intervals. You might wish to organise ages into 5 year periods: say 5-10, 11-15, 16-20, 21-25, and so on. Similarly, you could organise length of foot into groups of millimetres (centimetres), 1-10, 11-20, 21-30, 31-40, and so on. Note, however, that the size of shoe would count as discrete data - 3, $3\frac{1}{2}$, 4, $4\frac{1}{2}$, 5, $5\frac{1}{2}$ - as these are all free-standing and countable.

You could now present a graph showing the class intervals of ages, and, for example, the number of people doing certain things at those ages:

Histogram to show distribution of ages of television viewers

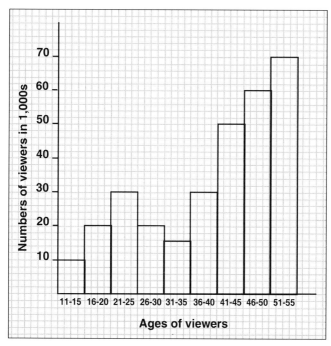

Note that, because the class intervals are all the same size (groups of 5), the representation on the paper as a graph needs to communicate the idea of the same size as well. We use the same number of squares on the graph paper to show the same size of grouping.

Presenting the data

For skill C3 you need to produce a line graph, or a bar chart, or a histogram.

> A line graph shows the relationship between variables.
> A bar chart shows the relationship between discrete data and frequencies.
> A histogram shows the relationship between continuous data and frequencies.

Line graphs

A basic kind of graph shows a positive or negative correlation - that is, a one-to-one relationship between two phenomena. For example, there would be a direct correlation between temperatures measured at Centigrade and at Fahrenheit.

Graph to show the relationship between Centigrade and Fahrenheit

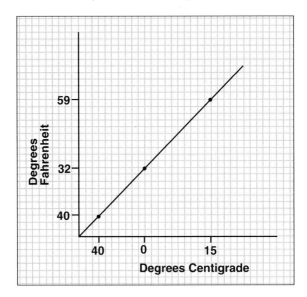

In psychology, however, we do not often use such a basic form, but tend to use line graphs to show the relationship between dependent and independent variables: that is, we are trying to establish a cause and effect relationship, and to show that the outcome - a change in the dependent variable - is a result of the manipulation of the independent variable.

In this kind of graph we usually put the dependent variable on the vertical axis and the independent variable on the horizontal axis. For example, in Britain it is normal that the temperature increases as summer approaches. We could say that the temperature is the dependent variable which depends on the time of year, the independent variable. Remember, the dependent variable depends on the independent variable.

Graph to show seasonal variability of temperature

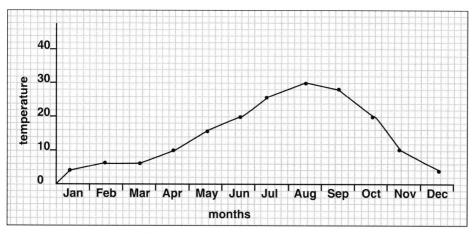

Note: this is continuous data.

We could conclude from this graph that there is a relationship between the independent and dependent variables, and that the independent variable causes the dependent variable.

> **We realise that this is an over-simplification, but it serves to show how line graphs may be used.**

This kind of graph is often used in exercises such as forecasting, or tracking, sales figures:

Graph to show sale of ice cream over year

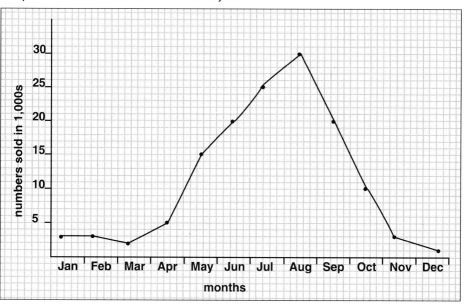

Note that often businesses are seasonally affected. This is why rises or falls in sales figures need to be related to times of year. You could say that the independent variable (time of year) had a direct influence on sales (dependent variable).

Exercise

Please draw a line graph to show the data to support the hypotheses that

1 the hotter the country is, the more desert it will have (variables: heat; amount of desert);

2 the more tourist attractions a resort can offer, the more visitors it will attract (variables: number of attractions; number of visitors);

Bar charts (also called Bar graphs)

Bar charts show the relationship between discrete data and frequencies. The variables being considered are all countable (discrete). Remember, the frequency (number of times a phenomenon occurs) is usually presented along the vertical (upright) axis; the variables (things we are studying) are usually presented along the horizontal (flat) axis:

Example of a bar chart

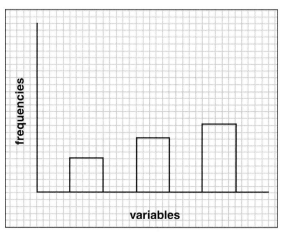

The information presented via the bars of the bar chart may be subdivided, forming compound bar charts: thus -

Example of a compound bar chart

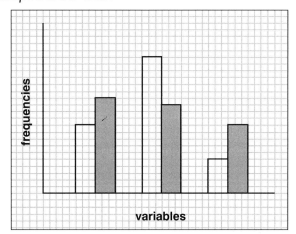

Note: the spaces between the bars of the bar chart do not need to be the same distance, unless we wish to show pictorially that there is some kind of value relationship.

An interesting form of bar chart is a pictogram, where the diagram uses pictures instead of columns. For example:

Chart to show numbers of different kinds of buildings

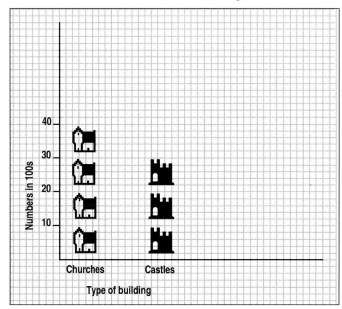

Histograms

Histograms show the relationship between continuous data and frequencies. The variables being considered are all part of a continuum, and the class intervals are all the same. So the bars in a histogram would all have the same width to indicate the value of the class interval:

Histogram to show height of students in a college

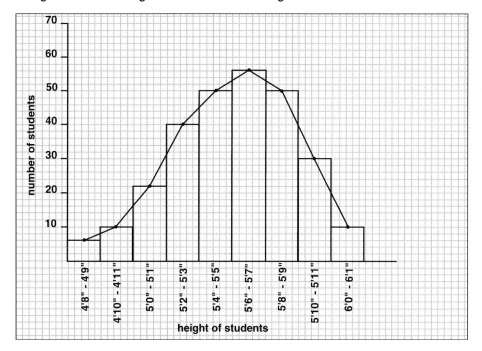

If you join the middle point of each bar you will get the frequency polygon, which usually takes a bell shape. The normal distribution curve indicates averages in populations, and tends to follow a common-sense idea of how frequencies actually do fall out - for example:

Histogram to show distribution of student age groups in Footle Adult and Continuing Education Centre

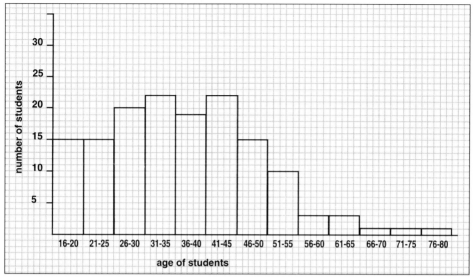

1   What is the total number of students in the Centre?
    How many are younger than 30?
    Which age group is largest?

2   Now draw either histograms or bar charts to show:

    The distribution of ages in your class;
    The distribution of shoe sizes in your class;
    How many people in your class like certain pop stars;
    How many people in your class like certain kinds of food.

3   How would you show the distribution of hobbies in your class?
    How would you show the average height of the people in your class?
    How would you show the average age of the people in your class?
    How would you show how many people like which different kinds of television programmes?

Calculating the percentage, median, mean, range and ratio

To obtain skill D2, you need to calculate two out of the following: percentage, ratio, median, mean and range. You need to show your workings, and show how your analysis of the data leads you to draw the conclusions that you do.

Percentages refer to parts of the data out of 100.
The terms, mode, median and mean, refer to central tendency.
The range refers to dispersion.
The ratio refers to the relationship between quantities.

Percentages

Percent means 'out of 100'. 1% = 1/100; 25% = 25/100; 100% = 100/100.
These fractions may be re-written like this: 1/100 = 0.01; 25/100 = 0.25; 100/100 = 1.00.
We can count the numbers of responses or behaviours that we observe (our data) and present them as percentages.

Central tendency

The Mode

(This is not specifically asked for by the NEAB, but this is how you calculate it.) This refers to the score or value that is most present in any list. For example, a class of 15 students take a test and get the following scores:

18, 16, 16, 18, 15, 14, 19, 18, 17, 18, 12, 15, 18, 16, 11

The mode in this case is 18, as this is the most commonly appearing figure.

The Median

This is the score gained by the middle person on our test. To find the median we rank the scores - that is, arrange them in order of size - and find the middle:

1	19
2	18
3	18
4	18
5	18
6	18
7	17
8	16
9	16
10	16
11	15
12	15
13	14
14	12
15	11

The median is the middle figure - 16.

The mean

The mean is another way of saying what we usually call 'the average'. The mean is probably the easiest value to calculate. Simply add up the scores and divide by the number of people taking the test. In our example,

$$19+18+18+18+18+18+17+16+16+16+15+15+14+12+11=241$$

$$241÷15=16.1$$

Ratio

This idea indicates the relationship between two sets of figures or two values; for example, we could talk about two men to every three women; or six responses from Group A to four responses to Group B.

Exercises

Find the mean, mode and median of the following groups of figures:

a. 7, 9, 10, 10, 11, 13, 14
b. 26, 28, 31, 31, 37, 37, 39, 52

Find the mean, modal and median height of the people in your class.

Find the mean, modal and median shoe size in your family.

EXERCISE

Dispersion

The range

The range is the number of scores between the top score and the bottom score. It tells us about the spread of scores, or their dispersion. A weekly test gives us the following marks for John and Jane.

	Week 1	2	3	4	5	6	7	8	9	10
Jim	18	18	19	20	13	12	18	17	16	18
Jane	19	16	15	18	17	16	15	19	13	18

We can see that the range of scores for Jim is 6 (18-12) and the range for Jane is also 6 (19-13). The range does not tell us which one is performing better overall, though, and for that we would need to take a more sophisticated measuring device called the standard deviation. That is, however, outside the scope of GCSE psychology.

Note How to rank when several people get the same score. We take the average of their positions - that is, sum their positions and divide by the number of persons:

Participant	Score	Rank
A	90	1
B	75	2.5
C	75	2.5
D	70	4
E	68	5

General reminders about coursework requirements

You need to show any two calculations out of the five mentioned here. Do not be put off by the idea that this is statistics. All you are doing is describing in easy pictures the information that you have gathered in your study.

All your graphical presentations should be done on graph paper. At least **ONE** presentation should be done by hand. The examiners are looking to see if you can handle calculations, not if you can get the right programme on the computer.

Labels - you must label all your axes absolutely clearly. It is not enough to put '%' or 'numbers' along an axis. You must write out the labels clearly and neatly. Titles should be clear and unambiguous. Do not be afraid of writing a long title.

Identify what kind of graphic you are showing. Write 'A bar chart to show ...' or 'A histogram to show ... '. If you do not label your work neatly and clearly, you might lose marks.

Finally, keep your work neat and attractive. Neatness is important in graphical representation, not only from an aesthetic point of view, but also because you are communicating in pictorial form the numerical information you have gathered. Neatness will not only help your examiner - it will also help you.

Answers to exercise on page 119

a.   mean   10.57
       mode   10
       median   10

b.   mean   35.125
       mode   31 and 37
       median   34

PART 5
INTERPRETING THE DATA

This section offers advice on writing up the report and presenting it for accreditation.

After all the hard research, it is now most important to get the presentation right. There are certain conventions applicable in writing up a scientific report.

Chapter 13 offers detailed guidance on writing up your report.

Chapter 14 looks at what the completed folder will look like cover to cover.

13 WRITING THE REPORT

Now you have done all the hard work of carrying out the study and gathering the data. The study is ready to be written up. What does the document look like?

In any professional exercise there is an accepted way of presenting a report. Psychology is no exception. If you stick to the following advice, you will help yourself to gain maximum marks.

The 'expanded' received format for a psychological enquiry (and for other social scientific enquiry such as sociology) is:

```
                    Title

Abstract
Introduction/aims
        Hypothesis
Method:   Design
          Subjects/participants
          Materials/apparatus
          Procedure

Results:  Description/summary
          Analysis/treatment

Discussion
Conclusion
References
Appendices
```

(Coolican, 1990)

At GCSE you are required to follow a modified format of this, and present your study under the following headings:

```
Introduction
Method
Results
Discussion
Conclusion
```

(see NEAB syllabus for 1995, page 16, paragraph 30).

You will find that there is a rough parallel between the skills list and the presentation of the report. The match is not exact, but it goes something like this:

Report	Skills
Title	
Introduction/Aims	A1,2,3,4,5,6,8,9,11,12
Hypothesis	A1
Method: Design	A2,3,6,7
Subjects/participants	B1
Materials/apparatus	A10
Procedure	A12, B2,3,4,5,6,7,8,9,10
Results: Description	C1,2,3,4,5
Analysis/treatment	D1,2
Discussion	E1,2,3,4,6,7,8
Conclusion	E5
References	
Appendices	

Your teacher has been asked by the Board to flag the skills. You can assist your teacher by flagging the skills that you think you have fulfilled in pencil. This means writing in 'A3' or 'B4' in the margin against the sentence or paragraph where you have demonstrated them. This information is also required on the skills list itself. Remember, you need to demonstrate each skill correctly only once throughout the entire folder.

Let's now look at the presentation of your report more closely. This is advice of a general nature. For detailed treatment of the individual skills, look back at Chapter 2.

Abstract

Writing an abstract does not gain you a mark, but it is normal procedure for a scientific report and lends an air of overall authority and professionalism. We would advise you to write one, although we would emphasise that it is not necessary at GCSE level.

An abstract summarises the whole report. It should be about $\frac{1}{2}$ side of an A4 page. An analogy is that if you want to see what a programme on television is about you would look in a preview such as 'The Radio Times'. There you would read about the main features of the programme. The abstract is something like this. It tells you what to expect in terms of content and form, and the main features of the study, including the outcome.

Introduction/aims

This section tells the reader what the purpose of the study is. When you are first planning your investigations, the question you need constantly to ask is, 'What do

I want to find out?' The introduction is the place to make a statement about what you want to find out - why you are undertaking the study in the first place, and why you are adopting this particular methodology. It is very important at this stage that you clearly state what your variables are: this is where you will be spelling out what kind of causal relationship you hope to demonstrate.

You should also specify here how your study is rooted in other similar issues; in other words, you should locate your own enquiry in the psychological literature, show what relevance that has for your own work, and indicate how your work might also make a contribution to the literature. This introductory section should take about $1-1\frac{1}{2}$ sides of A4.

The method

The introduction/aims says why you did the study, and locates those reasons within the wider general framework of psychological enquiry; the method now describes what you did and how you did it.

One of the criteria of excellence in writing a psychology report is that it may easily be read so that the study may be replicated. Replicability goes a long way to validating the study (it does what it says it is going to do) and ensuring its reliability (the study may be repeated with identical or matching results).

In order to achieve this clarity of reporting and so ensure that the study may be easily understood, transplanted and replicated, aim to develop a style that is clear, unambiguous and economical, as well as authoritative. This means telling a clear story, putting in all the detail. Do not assume that your reader knows what you are thinking. This is a very common fault in report writing. State the obvious. Sometimes the obvious may sound trivial, or a matter of common sense. It may well be, but you must say it all the same. Your written report is your only line of communication with your examiner. Use it well and to your advantage. State the obvious.

Design

The word 'design' is used in two separate ways: to denote the overall structure and format of the study - for example, is it an experiment or observational study? The word is also used in a specific sense in talking about experimental design. Both aspects are addressed in this section.

First give a clear outline of what kind of study it is. In talking through the form of the research, specify whether you had to use the idea of experimental design or not, which one you used, and why your choice was appropriate for the overall framework of the study. Your choice may be between independent samples, related measures and matched pairs. For example, if you are testing the speed of reaction of individuals under different conditions, you must have used a related measures design. Then say why this design was the appropriate one. The examiners are testing you here to see if you appreciate the different kinds of frameworks and approaches available to you in scientific enquiry, and if you can handle the machinery and appropriate techniques in putting them into operation.

Participants

There is now a requirement by organisations and agencies, such as the British Psychological Society, for the use of the word 'subjects' to be discontinued, and for the use of 'participants' to be standard practice. This is in response to the ethical issue of whether we do research ON people or WITH people. This is an essentially moral, ethical issue.

In writing about this aspect you need to address three points: the ideas of sampling, availability of resources, and suitable candidates.

You will need to specify what kind of sample you chose, and, as before, what you say here will show how you are aware that the overall shape and intention of your project has determined your choice of sampling technique. Therefore you have to say why you decided on this technique and discuss any implications there might be. Having explained why you chose your particular sampling technique, you then have to talk about the people who made up the sample, and show how they could be seen as representative of the wider population.

In talking about the people in the sample, you have to consider the general idea of availability of resources and the more specific aspect of whether the people you chose were suitable candidates. Availability of resources covers a number of aspects, including any necessary technology or equipment, and you need to mention that in your report. You have also to talk about accessing people to be sample members. If your study involves working with nurses, have you access to nurses? If you are giving a questionnaire to 30 people, are you confident that you can get 30 people to work with you? In conducting the study, clearly you did; but in the report you need to spell out that this was a consideration in your mind, and that you had an action plan as to how you could gain access to these people, and you must show how you implemented that action plan.

Then you need to show that you considered the suitability of your candidates. If you studied the relationship between married couples, were the people you interviewed all married? If your questionnaire was aimed at finding out the reasons for cognitive dissonance amongst alcoholics, would you have been able to interview or distribute the questionnaire to alcoholics? There are logistical issues involved here, as well as ethical and scientific ones. Among the people who you know will be prepared to support you in your study by acting as your sample, are there sufficient who really are suitable as representatives of the population you are wishing to investigate? If not, choose another area of study. Don't try to bend the facts or resources to fit an interesting hypothesis which you are unable to investigate fully. Keep it all coherent and under control.

The most easily accessible group to invite to be your sample is your class or group. You will probably opt for an opportunity sampling technique. If, however, your study is to investigate some aspect of the behaviour of psychology students, you might wish to go for a quota sampling technique. You must spell all this out in your report.

Materials/apparatus

You need to say what materials or apparatus were necessary. This can be very basic, from a clipboard and a pen, to very sophisticated, such as the equipment designed and manufactured by two students to test the sustainability of speed of manual dexterity of nightshift workers over a period of time.

Procedure

Here you need to tell the story of how you conducted the study, from its original planning to the implementation and testing of the hypothesis. Talk through the systematic steps of the enquiry, including any controls you introduced. Give a brief indication of the results and the statistical methods you used to describe and analyse them. This need not be a long section, but an indication of what you will deal with more fully in the next section. This 'procedure' section is really where your report will be judged most in terms of the potential replicability of the study. To repeat: one of the most common failings is that candidates do not state the obvious. You really must. As a check, when you have written your first draft, give it to a friend or family member and ask them to do the whole thing again in their mind. Would they understand everything they had to do? Or would they refer back to you to ask, 'How do I do this bit?' If you have problems with stating the obvious, put yourself in your reader's shoes by reading a manual about an unfamiliar discipline, such as operating a new computer programme, or following a new recipe. See how helpful very basic tips can be, and how important it is for the instructions or report to be presented in a systematic, easily comprehensible form. This is what you have to do in writing your report, especially the section on procedure.

The whole section on procedure could take about 2 sides of A4 paper.

Results

First, give a brief description and summary of the results - that is, review what you did to obtain the results (you explained this in detail in the section on procedure) and then specify what the scores, totals or other figures were. Refer your reader's attention to your record sheets, tables, or other materials for gathering and presenting data, and then place all of these sheets at the end of your report in the form of appendices, which are clearly labelled and numbered.

Second, explain what statistical tests you ran in order to analyse the results and draw conclusions from them. You need to calculate at least two out of the five operations - percentage, ratio, median, mean and range. You need to show your workings and show the results you arrived at. The raw data and workings may be part of the main body of the text, if it is succinct, or may be placed after the report as an appendix, if the material is substantial; but you do need to present a summary of the results in the main body of the text. As well as presenting the results in verbal form, you also need to put them into graphic form - in a graph, or a bar chart or a histogram. It is not enough just to present the graphics and let the figures speak for themselves. You have to explain the figures verbally and show how they will contribute to whether you retain or reject your hypothesis.

Discussion

The most important aspect of this section is to pick up on the original hypothesis. Are you keeping it or rejecting it? Why? State the hypothesis again, and show how your results led you to draw a relationship between the independent and the dependent variables. This means talking through the results in non-statistical language, and showing how they are leading you to draw certain conclusions. Discuss any trends that you might see or foresee from the analysis of your results. Here you can also identify any anomalous results - that is, any results that are odd or that you might not have anticipated. Discuss these briefly and say why you feel they might deserve further attention, perhaps in another study. If there are no anomalous results, you must say so in order to show that you understand the implications of the idea, and to gain a mark at skill D1.

Aim to evaluate your own method now to see if you have good reasons to believe your conclusions - and expect other people to do so, too. Criticise any aspects that might have been a bit weak. Most people recognise that their sample group was too small, or perhaps a questionnaire was not set out clearly enough. Sometimes people say that in retrospect they should have started from a different standpoint and adopted a different design altogether. You should offer your own evaluation of your work. Remember to try to give at least two points for improvement. Go beyond simply saying, 'We should have used more participants.' This alone will not impress examiners without ample justification.

You must relate your own work to the wider psychological literature. Quote or refer to some interesting reading from your psychology course book, or other books. You may also quote or refer to reports from newspapers, journals and magazines.

Finally, make some kind of general concluding statement about the results of your work and the contribution it has made to the literature - and we hope, to your own educational development as well.

References

You should include all references that you have cited in the report, including the sources in Domain E where you related your study to the wider literature.

There are several systems available for your use. The most common one takes this form:

Author's name (date), Title; Publisher.

Douglas, J.D. (1972), *Research on Deviance*; New York; Random House.

If you are referring to articles, you should write the title of the article either in plain text, or put single inverted commas round it.

There are no hard and fast rules for the style which you adopt for references. The rules for your own organisation are that you should be systematic, and, having decided on a format, you should stick to it.

Bibliogaphy

In a book, the references and the bibliography are usually the same thing. In a report like yours, the references indicate the works cited in the text. The bibliography indicates related useful reading. A bibliography is not essential, but some candidates like to include one. No skill marks are attached to this at GCSE level.

Here is an example of the difference between references and a bibliography. References refer to the texts you have actually cited in your report. For example, 'Coolican (1990) remarks that ... ': you would then put this reference in your references. However, if you found the work, say, of Cohen and Manion (1989) useful, but haven't actually referenced it, you might put that book in your bibliography. Most candidates choose not to write a bibliography.

Appendices

Appendices should be put at the end of the report, and should include all major rough workings or raw data. Some of the raw data may have gone into the main body of the text, in which case you do not need to produce it again in the appendices.

The appendices you are most likely to produce for your report are:

Appendix 1 - pilot(s) of questionnaire(s)
- questionnaire(s) (if not already in main body of text).

Appendix 2 - record sheet(s) from questionnaire observation schedules, survey material.

Appendix 3 - rough workings of calculations (if not already in the main body of the text).

Appendix 4 - reference material; if you have used, for example, newspaper articles, include a copy here if possible.

Appendix 5 - any other material not included so far.

Numbers of pages of appendices should follow on from the end of the reference or bibliography section. You should **not** begin your appendix again at a new page 1.

References

Cohen, L. and Manion, L. (1989), *Research Methods in Education* (Third Edition); Routledge.
Coolican, H. (1990), *Research Methods and Statistics in Psychology*; Hodder and Stoughton.

14 PRESENTING YOUR WORK

So you are ready to present your folder. What does it now look like? Here are some general guidelines to help you present your work in a way that is acceptable to the examination board and that does full justice to the many hours of work you have invested.

Size of paper

All work should be on A4 size paper.

Handwritten or typed?

You may do either. If you choose to handwrite, make sure that your work is neat, legible, well spaced out, and generally easy to read. Underline headings with a ruler, not by hand. Whether handwritten, typed or wordprocessed, certain conventions of presentation apply.

Spacing

Leave wide margins on either side, and top and bottom of the pages. If typed, use $1\frac{1}{2}$ or double spacing.

Headings

Keep all headings systematic, and develop a hierarchy, something like this:

1.0   TYPE A HEADINGS   main headings e.g. METHOD

1.1   Type B headings   for subheadings e.g. Projects

1.1.1. *Type c headings*   *for items within type B headings; e.g. sample groups*

You might also like to develop a headings notation such as

1.0   METHOD
1.1.   subjects
1.1.1. sample groups

or

1   Method
  (a)   subjects
      (i) sample groups

but this notation is not necessary, provided your headings are clear and self-explanatory.

It is up to you to guide your reader through your study, and to provide clear signposting as you go.

Structure of the report

Your report will be in three parts: the preliminary pages, the text, and the endmatter.

The contents of your folder should follow this format:

Front page: the 'Candidate Internal Assessment Form' provided by the examination board. Make sure that the skills you have earned are identified on this sheet with page numbers, and signed by your teacher.

Second page: the 'Coursework cover sheet' provided by the examination board which you must fill in accurately and sign at the bottom of the sheet.

Preliminary pages

The pages of the folder now follow in this sequence:

Title page (optional): this should contain the overall title of your work and your name. You may add a subtitle if it clarifies the main title.

Dedication (optional): if you wish you may write a dedication.

Contents page: You must write a contents page. This will list

(a) any preliminary matter;
(b) the part-titles or headings of the main text;
(c) the end matter (see below).

You should match the contents list with the page as you have numbered it in your folder.

Acknowledgements: you may acknowledge and thank anyone who has helped you. This may be in addition to the cover note which is a formal requirement of the examination board.

Text

Here you will present your studies. You should have written two, preferably three, separate studies. Each new study should begin as a new section on a new page, rather than be run on from the preceding one. It is possible that you might also have done some class-based exercises, perhaps to cover some of the skills which were not covered in your personal investigations. You should aim to present the complete studies first, and any exercises or part-studies after the completed pieces of work. If you write an abstract, the abstract for each study should go at the beginning of that study. You decide the order in which your studies are presented; there is no convention here.

Endmatter

This should include, in this order:

Any end-notes you may wish to include
References
Bibliography if desired.

The complete contents of your folder, then, may look something like this:

Length of your work

Each study should be about 1,000 words in length. This refers to the body of the text. It does not include diagrams, raw data, rough workings, pilot questionnaires, or any other appendix material, nor any title pages.

Numbering the pages

If you look in a book you will see that the preliminary pages have roman numerals at the top (i, ii, iii, iv ...) while the text is numbered in arabic numerals (1, 2, 3, 4 ...). You should number your pages in arabic (1, 2, 3 ...), with page 1 being your title page, bearing the title of the folder and your name. You will probably not number this page. It is a convention that the title page does not carry a number. Begin your numbering at page 2, which will be either your dedication page or your contents page. Number all pages in sequence, right through to the end of the folder. Do not begin a new page 1 for each new study. Put the numbers either at the top right hand corner or in the centre of the bottom of the page.

Compiling the folder

Put all pages together in sequence, with your coursework skills sheet on top, and endmatter material at the end. Attach them all together securely, either using treasury tags, or in a softback or flexible light plastic folder. Do not place your work in a hardback folder or ringbinder. Folders have to be sent to various parts of the country, and this would make things very expensive. Do not wedge your work into plastic wallets. You will not lose marks if you do, but you will not endear yourself to your examiners who have to negotiate their way around hundreds of submissions.

Spelling, punctuation and grammar
From 1994 onwards this will also be assessed in the coursework as well as in the written examination papers. Therefore it is worth taking the time and trouble to check through your work for errors before submitting it. The best way to deal with corrections of errors is not by the liberal use of correction fluid, but by allowing time to re-write pages if necessary.

The recommendations from the School Examinations and Assessment Council (SEAC) Code of Practice (1993) are these:

'Spelling, Punctuation and Grammar

For each written component, 5 per cent of the total marks available must be allocated to spelling, punctuation and grammar according to the three performance criteria below ... The marks must be included in the prescribed mark allocation for the paper.

Threshold performance

Candidates spell, punctuate and use the rules of grammar with reasonable accuracy; they use a limited range of specialist terms appropriately.

Intermediate performance

Candidates spell, punctuate and use the rules of grammar with considerable accuracy; they use a good range of specialist terms with facility.

High performance

Candidates spell, punctuate and use the rules of grammar with almost faultless accuracy, deploying a range of grammatical constructions; they use a wide range of specialist terms adeptly and with precision.'

Copyright material

You have already signed your coursework cover sheet to say that this is your own original work, except where stated. You should be aware that it is illegal to reproduce any one else's work without acknowledging your sources. It is of course permissible to cite or quote from sources, but you must acknowledge your source. The way to do this is: 'Gross (1992) suggests that ... ', or, if you are quoting direct: 'I agree with Freud that the id is the prime source of psychic energy: "It contains everything that is inherited, that is present at birth, that is laid down in the constitution - above all, therefore, the instincts" (Freud, 1964).'

Dates

Your work has to be with the moderator by 31st May. There are guidelines for samples to be sent, and your tutor will have these. They are updated regularly, so they are not reproduced here. Your Centre secretary will want to send the sample to the moderator by the middle of May, perhaps earlier, and will want all materials in good time to do the necessary paperwork and packing and posting. You can expect a submissions deadline for the end of April, or even the end of the spring term.

Your work will be sent to the moderator, if it is selected as part of the sample, or it will remain securely at the Centre. You may have your work back in October, or whenever the Centre is in a position to release it to you. The Centre must keep it pending any kind of query or appeals procedure about the marking following publication of the results, so do not press the Centre until at least mid-October for the return of your work. However, once submitted, coursework technically becomes the property of the examination board which has no legal obligation to return it. In practice, though, the boards make every effort to get the work back to the candidates.

What now?

By now you will probably be thinking, **'Never again!'** Not so.

This is just the beginning.

You ought now to be looking ahead and planning your future study. The next step after GCSE Psychology is 'AS' or 'A' level Psychology. There is a world of difference between GCSE and 'A' level, however. GCSE looks for basic skills in handling the ideas of social scientific enquiry. 'A' level looks for much deeper investigation, a wider range of coursework, and a more critical analysis of the literature. The syllabus itself is inspirational, and undertaking the course can be a challenging and highly rewarding exercise.

You could also take a lateral step and study for another GCSE subject area, such as Sociology. You have already mastered the skills of social scientific enquiry in your psychology project, so your workload will be substantially reduced.

Whatever you decide to do, please do keep on with your professional learning. You owe it to yourself to keep your mind open, to give yourself intellectual challenge, and to achieve on a continuing basis. The opportunities are available for continuing learning. Please use them in order to move yourself and the world to a better place.

PART 6

WORKED EXAMPLES FROM COURSEWORK

There now follow worked examples from coursework. All these extracts have appeared in real life. You are advised to study them carefully, and to see how the candidates presented their facts, information and their studies to gain maximum marks.

Example A: Taken from an observational study

Procedure   *B7*

Firstly I had to decide what subject to choose. I have been watching these particular soaps regularly and have always felt that both the verbal and non-verbal communication in English soaps is more negative than those shown in Australian soaps, so I decided to conduct my study in this field.

I waited until both storylines were at a stage where one of the principal characters had been hurt mentally, and therefore contained more negative verbal and non-verbal gestures, so as to obtain the main categories of behaviour. These categories were verbal insults or shouting, physical violence, and crying. Then I looked for some positive qualitites to match *A12* these with, such as the paying of compliments, showing affection, and laughing.

Time sampling had to be considered as 'Eastenders' runs for 30 minutes whereas 'Neighbours' only runs for 20 minutes. I used the whole of 'Neighbours', and edited parts of 'Eastenders' at random.

A pilot study was carried out and a table of categories drawn up. To make recordings of behaviour easier and more reliable, a tally chart was used.

I then watched both programmes and recorded the different types of behaviour on my tally chart (see tally chart, page 5).

RESULTS

A tally chart to show verbal and non-verbal behaviour categories recorded in 'Eastenders' and 'Neighbours'

A12
B10
B9

TYPE OF BEHAVIOUR	'EASTENDERS'	'NEIGHBOURS'
Verbal insults/shouting	⊪ ⊪ ⊪ ⊪ II	IIII
Physical violence	III	
Crying	II	
Compliments	I	⊪ I
Physical affection	I	⊪ II
Laughing/smiling	III	⊪ ⊪ IIII

C1 Table to show results of above tally chart to show verbal and non-verbal, negative and positive behaviour in 'Eastenders' and 'Neighbours'

C2

CATEGORIES	'EASTENDERS'	'NEIGHBOURS'
POSITIVE		
Compliments	1	6
Physical affection	1	7
Laughing/smiling	3	14
	Total 5	Total 27
NEGATIVE		
Verbal - insults/shouting	22	4
Physical violence	3	0
Crying	2	0
	Total 27	Total 4

Example B: Taken from a survey

Extraneous variables

A4 I have made my questionnaire anonymous so reducing any chance of recognition to participants. I felt that this would make them more honest in their answers.

A5 Noise, distraction or not having enough time to properly read the questionnaire could be a problem, so I will allow time for the participants to take the questionnaire away and return it later if any of these are a problem.

Apparatus

A questionnaire typed and photocopied (allowing enough spare to use in a pilot study). Graph paper to record results. *A10*

Procedure *B7*

First I had to decide which subject to use for my questionnaire. As my work involves health promotion I decided to write it on something that I was familiar with.

I first researched the subject, making sure that my statements and answers were correct.

After finishing the questionnaire it was important to pilot the questionnaire *B6* to 'iron out' any ambiguous or misleading questions, and to make sure that my participants clearly understood and were happy to complete the questionnaire. I picked six people of different ages, both sexes. This resulted in the changing of three questions and answers to include options that I hadn't considered before the pilot was carried out. After re-writing it, I had the questionnaire photocopied and sampled my participants (as described in 'Participants' section previously). I gave my questionnaire to 24 people.

It is important to remember good ethical practice, so I read out the following instructions to each participant:

'Would you mind taking part in a survey into self awareness of a healthy *B2* lifestyle? You needn't put your name at the top of the questionnaire as the results will remain anonymous and confidential. If you don't wish to answer a question please leave it blank. If you'd rather not participate then that's fine. *B8* Thank you very much.'

Everybody I asked filled in my questionnaire and answered every question.

After the participants had finished I de-briefed them by saying, *B3*

'Thank you very much. Your answers will help me to determine a hypothesis on people's awareness of a healthy lifestyle.'

Discussion

The first pattern that is most noticeable is that which my 2nd hypothesis *E2* shows to be correct. That is that women are more health conscious than men. From the lowest score of 33% to the highest of 100% the average female *E1* score was 78% and the average male score 67.12%; that is an average mark of 28.1 out of 36 for the women compared to 24.1 for men.

As for my other hypothesis that the younger generation is more health conscious than the older, the 40 year olds scored the highest out of the four age groups. They scored 76.4%; the 50 year olds came last with 67.6%; the 20 year olds came second with the 30 year olds coming third.

One reason for the 30 year olds not scoring as well as expected may be that this is the age group most likely to be extremely busy with a young *E4* family with associated financial worries. A lot seemed to suffer with stress related problems, and also smoked and were overweight.

Possibly the 40 year olds are being kept in check by their teenage children. It does seem today to be fashionable to be health conscious and fit among teenagers. Surveys have shown that more and more teenagers, especially girls, are vegetarian, for example.

Then we come to the lowest scores, the 50 year olds. Perhaps this could be attributed to a less health conscious society of the 1960s.

B5

QUESTIONNAIRE

SELF AWARENESS OF A HEALTHY LIFESTYLE

HOW IMPORTANT IS IT TO ESTABLISH A HEALTHY LIFESTYLE, TO PROTECT AGAINST THE DEVELOPMENT OF PROBLEMS LIKE HEART DISEASE IN LATER LIFE?

I WOULD BE MOST GRATEFUL IF YOU COULD COMPLETE THE FOLLOWING QUESTIONNAIRE FOR ME.

THANK YOU.

Age ....   Male/Female

1. Do you smoke?

   (A) Yes.
   (b) Yes, but I would like to give up.
   (c) No.

2. Smoking can double your risk of dying from a heart attack.

   (a) True.
   (b) False.
   (c) I don't know.

3. What do you have on your toast?

   (a) Butter.
   (b) Low fat spread.
   (c) Varies.

4. What type of bread do you eat?

   (a) White.
   (b) White or brown - it varies.
   (c) Brown.

5. How do you feel about artificial additives in foods?
   (If you never shop, how would you feel if you did do the shopping?)

   (a) Always check the labels or make a conscious effort to avoid them.
   (b) Just pick it up and put it in the trolley.
   (c) I am aware of the additives but never read the packet.

6. Do you take exercise?

   (a) Rarely.
   (b) Sometimes.
   (c) Regularly.

7. Do you think you are overweight for your height?

   (a) Probably. I don't weigh myself very often.
   (b) Yes, I am, and I know that I should lose some weight.
   (c) No.

8. How much alcohol per week do you drink?

   (a) Up to 10 pints (or equivalent).
   (b) Over 10 pints.
   (c) Occasionally or never.

9. Could you happily go down to the pub for an hour and just drink non-alcoholic drinks?

   (a) I suppose so. I wouldn't find it much fun though.
   (b) No, I'd sooner not bother.
   (c) Yes, no problem.

10. What is the maximum weekly recommended intake of alcohol for men?

    (a) 14 units.
    (b) 21 units.
    (c) Don't know.   (1 unit = pint or equivalent)

QUESTIONNAIRE

QUESTIONNAIRE

11. How many of the following do you suffer from?

Please tick

(1) guilt when relaxing
(2) awake worrying at night
(3) difficulty in decision making
(4) sweaty palms
(5) dry mouth
(6) difficulty in concentrating
(7) impatience
(8) irritability

Please add up ticks

(A) Less than 2
(b) 2 - 4
(c) More than 4

THIS IS THE LAST QUESTION

12. Has answering this questionnaire made you think any deeper about your health and lifestyle?

(a) Yes, I may think about changing a few things.
(b) No, not really.
(c) Yes, but I doubt if I will make any changes.

THANK YOU VERY MUCH

SCORING

Question	1	2	3	4	5	6	7	8	9	10	11	12
A		1	3	1	1	3	1	1	2	2	2	2	3
B		2	1	3	2	1	2	2	1	1	3	2	1
C		3	2	2	3	2	3	3	3	3	1	1	2

Example C: Taken from an experiment

TITLE: An experiment to show the effect of category headings on the recall of a list of words.

Introduction

There are many methods used to help us to remember and also to try and improve our memory. One of these methods is to provide cues to enable us to retrieve our memories by linking one part of our memory with another. This experiment is to show how we use these cues, in this case to remember a list of words using category headings.

An appropriate sampling technique representative of the whole population would be a random sample, meaning to set up a situation in which *A8* anyone in the population has an equal chance of being selected. Although this method would be the most appropriate, it would not be easily employed.

Hypothesis

A list of categorised headings will aid recall as opposed to having no labels *A1* at all.

Method

An independent measures design will be used in this experiment, this measuring two separate groups who are both asked to recall a list of words *A6* previously given to them. However, only one group has a piece of paper with category headings on it, whilst the other group has no headings on their pieces of paper. Both groups have to recall and write down the words remembered.

This is the most suitable design to use, as repeated measures would mean *A7* that the subjects may remember more words as they had run through both *A11* sides of the experiment. Matched pairs would have worked well, but this requires pre-testing and would have taken too long to set up.

Therefore, as all the subjects used in this experiment are of similar ability (being GCSE evening class students), the independent measures design would be quite fair and justifiable for this experiment.

Independent variable

The independent variables are the category headings. *A2*

Dependent variable

The results - the number of words recalled. *A3*

Extraneous variables

A4 The time given for the participants to see and write down the words - should be equal.

Noise would have affected concentration - peace and quiet needed.

Both groups should take part at the same time.

A5 Making sure both groups had a small sum to calculate in their heads after seeing the words so as to clear the short term memory.

Participants

A8
B1
An opportunity sample could be used (meaning to use whoever I can get) but in this case the population that I am using for this experiment has been narrowed down to evening class students, so the sample used is a 'cluster sample', meaning a ready made group who have come together by chance.

There are 23 participants, 11 in one group and 12 in the other, all female apart from one male.

Apparatus

A10 The resources needed for this experiment are an overhead projector, 32 words to flash up for 3 seconds per word, a stop watch to time this, 12 pieces of paper with category headings and 11 pieces of paper without labels.

Procedure

Firstly the two lists of words were drawn up, 32 in all, and these included vegetables, sports, parts of the body, animals, musical instruments, insects, weapons and fruit, but in no set order.

When the subjects were all sitting down they were given standardised instructions (see end of procedure section).

I then gave the group a small pre-test by putting a few words up on the screen for 3 seconds each, just to ensure that everyone could see clearly *B7* and understood exactly what was expected of them (see Appendix 2).

I then proceeded with the experiment, flashing the words from an overhead projector onto the screen for exactly 3 seconds per word (see Appendix 3). After this I gave the class a calculation to work out in their heads, to clear their minds of any short term memory.

The class were then given pieces of paper on which to write down as many words as they could recall. Half the class had category headings on their sheets (see Appendix 4), and the other half had nothing on theirs (see Appendix 5).

The subjects were given 3 minutes of recall to list as many words as they could.

The sheets were collected in and the class de-briefed (see end of procedure section).

Standardised Instructions:

'Firstly, thank you for agreeing to take part in this experiment, although there is no obligation to do so, and you have the right to withdraw now. The results will be confidential.

This experiment involves a list of 32 words which will be flashed up on the screen for 3 seconds per word. You will then have 3 minutes to recall and write down as many of these words as you can remember, on sheets which I will then hand out.

Does everyone understand these instructions?

Thank you.'

B2

De-briefing

'This experiment was to find out if headings will aid recall. Half of you had categorised headings on the sheets of paper I gave you, on which to write the words you recalled, but the other half of you had no labels.

The results will remain confidential.

Thank you very much for taking part.'

B3

Results

Table to show results

- the first column shows the results of the subjects without labels to aid recall;
- the second column shows the results of the subjects who had category headings.

PARTICIPANTS	(NO LABELS) SCORES	PARTICIPANTS	(WITH LABELS) SCORES
1	10	12	23
2	14	13	14
3	7	14	10
4	14	15	11
5	13	16	16
6	6	17	19
7	6	18	14
8	14	19	11
9	16	20	16
10	18	21	16
11	20	22	5
		23	24
	138		179

B4

Average	12.5	Average	14.9
Median	14	Median	15
Mode	14	Mode	16

C1
C2
D2

Graphs to show results - see Appendix (1)

Discussion

E1
E2

The results clearly show that the participants who were given labels scored higher marks, the average mark being 12.5 in the group with no labels, as opposed to 14.9 in the group with category headings to help them. This would indicate to me that my hypothesis that labels aid recall is correct, that category headings are an aid to recall. In psychological terms, the reason for this was that the labels provide us with 'cues' (meaning something which gives us an idea or hint). Therefore, giving us the right cue helps us to retrieve our memories, in the case of this experiment the 'cue' being the labels.

E6

D1
I found one anomalous result in my data, the one person who scored the lowest but who had category headings to aid recall.

E7
I didn't find any problems in doing the experiment, but I may have been able to obtain a more conclusive result had I had time to use matched pairs - this would have meant that my participants having been pre-tested would have had similar memory recall capabilities.

Tulving and Pearlstone

E8 In 1966 these psychologists conducted a similar experiment to show how important cues could be.

They gave their participants lists of categorised words to remember. The lists were taken away and the participants split into two groups and asked to recall the words. Half were given sheets with labels, the others sheets without.

The group given the cues (labels) recalled more words.

Conclusion

E5 The results justify my hypothesis that labels will aid recall as opposed to no category headings to give us memory cues. However, it would be difficult to generalise from these results because the sample is not representative of a wider population.

Appendix 1

Graph to show results of experiment to show that labels aid recall

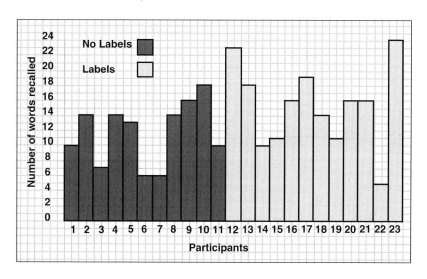

C3
C4
C5

Appendix 3

cucumber	goat
cow	carrot
butterfly	dagger
flute	face
lime	softball
brain	plum
fishing	centipede
moose	revolver
broccoli	yam
mosquito	guitar
sword	lemon
tuba	skiing
hand	flea
shotgun	leopard
table tennis	cherry
harp	

Appendix 2

test
can
you
read
this
????

(Roediger, Rushton, Capaldi and
Paris (1984), *Study Guide to
Accompany Psychology*;
Little, Brown and Co.)

Appendix 4

Recall as many words as you can using the labels to aid your recall.

Vegetables

Yellow _____

_____

Green _____

_____

Musical instruments

Wind _____

_____

String _____

_____

Sports

With balls _____

_____

Without balls _____

_____

Insects

Flying _____

_____

Creeping _____

_____

Parts of the body

Internal _____

_____

External _____

_____

Weapons

Stabbing _____

_____

Shooting _____

_____

Animals

Wild _____

_____

Domesticated _____

_____

Fruits

Citrus _____

_____

Non-citrus _____

_____

Appendix 5

Recall as many words as you can in any order you find convenient.

EVALUATION

We hope you enjoy using this book, and that you will learn much that will help you to get a good grade in your examinations.

We have learnt a good deal in writing it. We are aware already that we could have done things better in a number of instances; that the book might benefit from self-study exercises; that we might have found better examples, and so on. Books are never completely finished, because they can always be improved and refined in order to meet their readers' needs more effectively.

With a view to revising any parts that are less useful, and introducing new aspects that might be more useful, we ask you to let us know your opinion about the text. If you have any comments about strengths or weaknesses, any ideas as how the text might be improved, please let us know. We will respond with gratitude.

You can reach us in care of Hyde Publications, 57 Exeter Road, Bournemouth, Dorset, BH2 5AF.

Jean McNiff and Mike Stanley

Index